Targeted at Birth

By: Qunetta Davis

TARGETED AT BIRTH

Copyright © 2021 by Qunetta Davis

Table of Contents

Chapter 1

One night Sanity was sitting in the front room with her little brother Tim when Willie started yelling.

"I'm so sick of all of y'all talking about what y'all want to do. Ain't no damn body got no money to be throwing away and money don't grow on trees," yelled their dad from down the hall of the three-bedroom small home. "This home is shared with multiple family members with barely enough room for y'all to sleep. You don't hear Kiesha and Joe talking crazy like that because they know better. Joe is going to be the one making all of the money because he plays ball well and that's the only damn thing he will be able to do. Thanks to your Grandma for spoiling him like a baby, that boy ain't going to ever grow up if she don't stop that. I see y'all ain't got nothing to say. Like I said, get over it. When y'all get grown enough to get a job and get y'all own money then y'all can say what y'all want, but I know I am not paying for nothing. That's a waste of time sitting in here talking about singing. Sanity, how the hell do you want to sing? You must be crazy to think I'm going to let you go to a damn studio as young as you are."

Sanity said, "But Willie I love music and me and my friends love singing." Their dad had a way with words. It was very harsh, and Sanity thought that was the worst way to show kids love. It did not feel like love when he would yell and curse every day, sometimes for such little things. He would say, "you think you're going in a damn studio around all those boys that don't want nothing but some ass from you in return." She would just wait till she was by herself and cry because he didn't know that she was not that type of girl. Her dad was too overprotective of all of them. It was to the point where they had already planned their escape long before anyone could ever see it coming. There were nights they all felt as if Willie was being too hard on them. However, only one of them was willing to stand up to him and that was Tim. He would always say, "man I'm about to flip; I'm going to have to say something to him."

"No Tim, because if you say something to him all of us are going to get in trouble and you know how that goes. If one of us get in trouble, then all of us get in trouble."

"Well Sanity if we don't say something then this shit going to keep on happening." It came to a point when Tim knew the consequences but did not care, he just wanted to be heard. Tim looked at her and said, "sis you going to make it. I promise you're going to make it. Your voice will take us right on up out of here because I'm going to make sure that." A loud deep voice came from down the hall, "you ain't grown Tim. I'm going to show you, you ain't grown since you around there talking all crazy."

Of course, she wanted to defend him, but she was too scared to stand up for him just as much as he was standing up for her, so she cried because she knew Tim was going to get a whipping for speaking out and expressing how he truly felt about her dreams. Even though Tim was much younger than her, he still knew the right words to make her feel like she was worthy and the best at what she loved doing, which was singing. "You around here talking under your breath like you run this damn house I go out and I bust my ass every day to make sure y'all have food on the table and a roof over y'all heads. Just because I'm not allowing your sister to think she going to take her hot ass to a studio around a bunch of niggas then so be it. I already know how hot she is, just want to get around a bunch of boys."

"But Willie that ain't even the case I just love music and you know I love it. I am right here singing all the time. Why do you always think somebody just wants to be around a bunch of boys? I'm not even like that and you should know that." Their dad was not trying to hear that. He just thought that every guy that saw her would do something to harm her and that was his way of being extremely overprotective.

Him being that way only made her curious. They could barely have friends over to the house or go over to people's houses. If they didn't get in the house by the time the streetlights came on, they would get in trouble for disobeying his rules. When they tried to have friends over, they would all stand on the porch playing games and listen to Sanity fool around with music. They knew that if one of them made it out of the hood, then all of them would. They knew Sanity was the type of person that would not leave anyone behind. As long as she had it then everyone else had it. Even though those were the happiest moments of their lives, their dad would still come home after working all day and fuss at them.

They never understood why all of their friends'
parents were not as strict as Willie, but they knew
he only wanted to protect them, but in a way that
they were too young to understand.

Chapter 2

Their friends would ask them why they called their dad by his name. They said their parents would kill them if they did that. They thought that the reason they called him by his name was because he was very mean, however that wasn't the case. They called him by his name because their grandparents also lived in the house, and because they heard everyone call them mom and dad and that's just what they learned to do. They thought that their grandparents were the best they could have ever asked for. They were treated as if they birthed them their selves. Their grandfather didn't talk much but grandmother was always a listening ear and they loved her so much. She was there through anything they went through in life and never judged them, not once.

Their mother Catherine never paid them much attention. She would always wait until she got Sanity's and her siblings' allowance from Willie to spend it on things for herself. She got the girl's hair done once every month, if that, but made sure her hair was done every week out of the kid's money. During Sanity's younger years, Catherine never had a job. She depended on their father's paycheck, which was a lot of stress on him. Sanity started to believe that was the reason he was so angry all the time. He had to pay all of the bills by himself along with Big Momma and their grandfather. Big Momma's only income was her Social Security checks and that together made sure that they kept their heads above water. They struggled a lot even with the three incomes; it still wasn't enough to make ends meet.

They were less fortunate and didn't have a lot of the things that their friends at school had. It was embarrassing. They didn't know what to do some days and all they could do was cover up the pain by trying to dress the best they could so they wouldn't get picked on. However, that didn't stop Sanity from being bullied. A few years into her school years, she wanted to ask Catherine how she could let Willie fuss at them all the time over nothing. Yelling at them because taking care of them was so overwhelming. But she stayed in her room and didn't say anything.

Sanity knew if she said anything to her mother about it, she would only go back and tell Willie and it would have gotten all of them in trouble. By that time, she was tired of getting yelled at. Getting up going to school was hard because she was tired of feeling like she was not pretty enough. Sanity spent a lot of time pointing out her own flaws. She blamed their mother Catherine, because she felt she should have sat her down and taught her how to take better care of herself. Saying something to her would have been pointless because she never spoke up for them or even had conversations with them. Sanity started to feel like she was the only one who saw the wrong in what Catherine was doing.

Sanity and Tim always had a very tight bond and their relationship with their mother was something they spoke on a lot. They tried to figure out why she didn't really interact with them and why she didn't talk to them like a mother should have. It was safe to say they were on their own if they wanted to make a change and have a better chance at life. Sanity and Tim knew they couldn't trust speaking on those matters to anyone.

Laying on the couch next to Tim were some of the best moments in Sanity's life because they had some of the best conversations. They could talk about anything, especially their big dreams. They could manifest it if they put their all into it. They had many conversations on why their mom was so distant and why she allowed so many things to go on in their lives. They would agree that they didn't deserve to live like that. If only she would have tried to work and help Willie, then he wouldn't have had so much to fuss about. Their lives would have been better and more at peace. "Tim I just don't see how we are going to be able to do this," Sanity said. "We don't have no money, can't go nowhere, and we don't have anybody to talk to about music. We might make the biggest mistake of our life." Even if they made it, it would have been hard for them because their parents would have had to sign papers because they're too young. So, she asked him, "what do we do next?"

"Girl I'm not worried about that," Tim said. "Just watch this we are going to make it I promise you take my word. I don't care how. You know it's people out there waiting for somebody like you to come into the studio. I promise, you should stop worrying man we gotta get out of this. I'm sick of all of this yelling every day for no reason." He said, "all we do is sit in the house and listen to them yell back and forth." Big Momma always thought that

Willie was being too hard on the kids. But she knew, like everyone in the house, that Catherine would never in a million years stand up for anything. In her eyes it was right. All of the kids had a don't care type of attitude towards her. After a while, Sanity started caring more about singing than she did school and to her, school was pointless. Catherine was never at any of the parent teacher conferences and if she was it was very dry. The teachers started to wonder if something concerning was going on inside of their household. Clearly, they didn't think Catherine understood that Sanity was going down a long dark road of destruction.

Chapter 3

When Sanity walked through Big Momma's room with her hair looking a mess she said, "I don't know why your momma doesn't keep up with your hair. Hell, she gets a check every first of the month and your dad is giving her money every Thursday so you ain't got no business walking around here looking like that." This is when Sanity learned that Catherine was getting a welfare check for them. All that the girls got out of the check was a meal from the local neighborhood food mart that they caught a taxi to when Catherine felt like taking them. However, it didn't bother their older sister Keisha much about what was going on. She didn't speak on it, but Sanity knew it had to have caused her the same pain as it did all of them.

Keisha learned how to do her own hair and made her clothes look like they were worth something. Sanity admired her for that. Doing hair was never Sanity's thing. Singing and dreaming of becoming an actor always was. They had to be in the bed at a certain time every night. She would pray while she tried to find something to wear to school the next day, so she didn't get looked at as the kid that came from nothing. Sanity didn't complete her homework and didn't pay attention in a few of her classes because she didn't have the energy to focus on school and no one made sure she did it anyway.

She knew that Catherine did not care about being a mother. It wasn't supposed to be like that Sanity knew this. When you have kids, it is a priority to take care of them. She just didn't feel that love or that sense of care from Catherine at all. She couldn't think of one time that Catherine asked her if she had any homework or if she needed help with it. She never asked those questions and that is what Sanity needed from her. Sanity didn't have the energy to ask her why she wasn't involved in her life as she should have been. All Catherine cared about was making sure that she looked good while not knowing her children were slipping away. Sanity knew she was worth more and wanted more out of life so she figured if she channeled her energy in another direction then she could give her sisters and brothers everything they never had.

Even though Willie was what the old folks called "a hellraiser," he was a great provider for everyone in the home. Yeah, there were certain things that they didn't understand about him, and there were certain things they didn't like about him; however, they did know he gave Catherine everything she needed to provide for their children. She failed them and was not loving to them. Sanity knew what real love felt like because she got it from Big Momma, their grandfather, and Willie. The only thing that was missing was the love she should have gotten from her mom. In her mind, she always felt as if Catherine was not happy being mother to them. She wasn't ready since she had them at a very young age. By the time she was eighteen, she gave birth to all five of her children. Sanity figured if Catherine aborted her then life would have been much better for her. That was how Catherine made her feel. She remembered telling her mom how she wanted to sing and act but she would always blow it off as if her dreams didn't matter. She never spoke about it to anyone because they would never understand what she wanted to do in life.

Sanity never got to attend any school events because her family didn't have the funds. Catherine never showed any interest in anything that was going on at the school and that also led Sanity down a very dark path of destruction. She never spoke on it because her voice was never heard so it wouldn't make any sense to tell anyone how she felt. Sanity held it all in hoping and praying that one-day things would get better. Hoping that her mother would finally see she had five talented kids that wanted to do something with their lives. They wanted to give their mother a better life, but she never supported any of their dreams. All she did was blame them for coming into the world so early, as if they could have helped that. When their birthdays would come around, they never had parties like everybody else. That was never going to happen.

Chapter 4

Catherine's actions showed them that they ruined her life, and she hated that they were brought into the world. If she had it her way, she would have aborted all of them just so she could have lived a better life. Sanity watched Catherine day in and day out admiring her beauty only to be treated like she wasn't beautiful enough to be her daughter. If only she knew Sanity looked up to her and she wanted to be loved in a way that she had never been before. Big Momma, her grandfather, and Willie loved her dearly and they showed her. Sanity was so surprised that Catherine couldn't give them the same love that she got from her grandparents in return.

Big Momma had nine children but that didn't stop her from showing each and every one of her kids that she loved them and would do anything to provide for them even though she never worked. Sanity's grandfather got up every morning and worked countless hours to help provide for the family inside of the small home. Every dollar he gave Big Momma and she made sure her grandchildren would be okay even when it came to something as small as a cheap field trips for school that they couldn't go on. Catherine's answer would always come off as if they were frustrating her for asking. It was always, "I don't have any damn money," but yet they would see her buy everything to enhance her beauty such as hair weave, getting her nails done, and buying new outfits. While she would do this, her children were still putting together clothes they had to make them look worth wearing.

Sanity's eighth grade year in middle school was so exciting for her because Catherine allowed her to get her nose pierced making her one of the first in that grade to have a nose piercing. That made her feel a little prettier because of the new attention just for having a piercing. It wasn't allowed at school, but Catherine wouldn't have known because she wasn't active in their school lives. In every class the teachers would tell Sanity she wasn't allowed to have a nose piercing at school, but she would ignore them. Not for a second Sanity thought to herself that she would remove it when she was finally getting attention.

At that point, she became rebellious. Everything they asked her to do she didn't do. This gave her attention and it got to the point where she would get in trouble for disobeying the school rules and skipping out on class for not caring. Her behavior attracted people that were doing some of the same things, and this became the type of friends she hung out with. It was fun for her and felt good. She felt like the people's parents she was hanging out with showed her lots of love, so she was willing to do whatever it took to feel like someone loved her more than her own mother. The only fear Sanity had at that point in her life was getting suspended and Willie giving her a whipping because that's something he didn't play about at all.

Sanity always came up with an excuse for the things she did at school to get suspended. Sanity's suspensions would always begin with "you cannot return to school until a parent brings you back." Of course, Willie couldn't take her back because he had to work Monday through Friday during the school hours. She needed to return back to school so that left Catherine. Nothing that happened to them mattered to her unless it was beneficial for her like getting a welfare check for them. The only question Catherine would ask Sanity was why she kept doing the things that she was doing. Her favorite question was "Sanity do you have a mental problem or are you stupid or something?" She would yell and say "you got a damn problem just like your damn daddy. You will never be nothing if you keep on doing this." Not once did she ask Sanity what she could do to help her. Catherine failed to ask Sanity if she had something she needed to talk about. All she did was belittle her and told her she would only be just like Willie.

If Catherine only knew Sanity was crying out for attention from her. All of them acted out in their own way. For example, Tim chose to hang out with friends all the time at a very young age and not come home. From him and Sanity's conversation, he was tired of being home hearing everyone fuss all the time. However, they couldn't go to Catherine to talk to her about anything. Five siblings shared the same parents not knowing how to look out for each other because they were never taught to love and be there for one another. Their brother Joe, on the other hand, kept very quiet. He played sports and thought that was his ticket out just like Sanity did when it came to music and acting. He gave it his all. He would be in the local newspaper headlines for football and basketball. He was great at what he did, and he worked hard. His siblings supported him, but

he rejected the support because they weren't giving
him what he wanted when he wanted it. They
would walk past each other as if they were strangers.
Out of all of the adults who lived in their home, only
a few were on board with teaching the
siblings speaking to each other, loving each other,
and being there for each other was important as a
family.

Chapter 5

Sanity and Joe were close in age, so they attended the same school. Sanity heard from everyone around the school, "your brother this, your brother that, your brother is going to be a star." Sanity always felt in her heart he was a star. She rooted for him in silence and found ways to attend every game because of course, no one else ever showed up to support him. There was one major event when Catherine was recognized as the mother of the year because she knew there would be coaches from all over the world there. Sanity would stay after school for the games not knowing how she would get home. She and her friends would walk, and Tim would meet her there even if he had to walk miles. He would make sure he was always there to support Joe as well. However, Joe didn't show much appreciation. It didn't bother them because they knew with the type of family they were brought up into, attention wasn't something they always received. Sanity felt weird around school. It was as if she and Joe weren't related because they would walk past each other as if they didn't even see one another. It was very noticeable they were related.

Keisha, as the older sister, did her own thing as if nothing ever bothered her. She acted as if not getting that love from their mom was okay, but Sanity knew deep down inside Keisha had to have been feeling the same pain. Keisha hung out with a group of girls at school that Sanity and her friends called the "badazz crew." It seemed as if they ran the whole school and Sanity's two very close cousins were a part of it. Sanity assumed this was how Keisha was dealing with what was going on inside of their home. One night after one of Joe's games, Sanity was in the house trying to do different things with her hair in the mirror. She figured if she could have done anything to make herself feel better. Burying the pain was all she wanted to do. Sanity was willing to do anything just to feel better about herself.

      The first of the month came around again. "Sanity," Catherine yelled. "Come here for a second." Sanity walked to her mom's room very slowly because she did not know what the conversation was about. She figured she was calling her to point out more flaws or maybe even tell her to "take that stupid ass look off of her face and stop looking like her daddy Willie." Surprisingly she said, "I'm going to take you to get your hair done tomorrow and I want you to go somewhere with me, but you better not say shit about where we're going just put something nice on." In that moment Sanity finally felt as if her acting out had finally gotten her mom's attention. The attention she always prayed for from her mom felt life changing. Catherine heard her cry. Sanity was up all night because she was excited for their mommy-daughter date the next morning. In the back of her head, she tried to figure out how she would tell Tim Catherine wanted to take her out. Her mom told her not to say anything about it. Sanity thought it would ruin her chances of ever going out and having a one on one with Catherine.

Chapter 6

In the small three-bedroom house live two of Sanity's older cousins and two of Catherine's older brothers. One of the cousins who Sanity was very close with is TJ. TJ and Sanity were inseparable. Every time he would have to make a grocery store run for Big Momma, he always asked Sanity if she wanted to go, so that was her way of getting some fresh air away from all the cussing and fussing. She would always be ready to jump up and go and didn't care how far the walk was. The family had their suspicions of TJ being on drugs and Sanity heard a lot of conversations behind TJ's back but that didn't stop the love that she had for him. Sanity didn't feed into the rumors because she felt she was loved by a cousin but not her mom.

Her cousin TJ always came around with a guy he was with daily named Jimmy. Jimmy was tall, handsome, and had a light brown complexion. He looked like the player type, but Jimmy was also very nice to everyone in their family, and he would always joke around and play around with all of the kids. Sanity got close to Jimmy and there were times that TJ, Sanity, and Jimmy would walk to the store for Big Momma. These were some of the best moments of Sanity's life because they paid her a lot of attention, played around with her, and asked her about school. They would play pranks and jokes on each other all the time. Sanity noticed the more Jimmy came around Catherine would be extremely nice to her. Sanity also noticed Catherine fussed back with Willie a little more than usual. She finally started to stand up to him because she knew that he would always argue but never put his hands on her.

Catherine smiled more and did her hair in different styles even more than she ever had. Sanity woke up the next morning and felt like a kid in the candy store She was happier than she had ever been in life to finally get to bond with Catherine. A taxi pulled up and blew the horn for them to come out. Catherine yelled for Sanity to come on. Sanity got dressed as fast as she could and pulled her hair back in a ponytail with a huge smile on her face big enough to light up the room. Sanity and Catherine jumped into the back seat of the taxi. Catherine looked at Sanity and said, "I will get your hair done another day okay?" Sanity looked back at her and said, "okay well where are we going?"

Catherine said, "remember I told you I wanted you to go somewhere with me?"

"Yeah," Sanity said with a puzzled look on her face.

"Well, I'm going to see a friend of mine, but you can't say nothing about it to anyone you hear me?"

Still feeling so confused Sanity said, "okay" and then stared out of the window of the taxi. She just did not understand what was going on, she knew it did not feel right at all.

"Okay is this your stop," The taxi driver said to Catherine.

"Yes, this is. Thank you so much I will call you back when we are ready," she replied. Sanity was looking around out of the taxi window and asked, "who lives here?"

"Don't worry about that, just come on and remember what I told you. Keep your mouth shut." Catherine said, "It ain't nobody business where we go you hear me Sanity?"

The tone Catherine used kind of hurt Sanity's feelings because it was much different from when she spoke to her the night before asking her to go with her. Sanity wondered why her attitude changed whenever she would ask questions about where they were going. Sanity knew something was not right; she just couldn't pinpoint what it was. All she knew was the apartments they pulled up to were very rundown, and no one ever had anything good to say about it in the small country town where they were from. It was known as one of the worst projects in the town but yet still wondering why they were there left young, confused Sanity still puzzled. Sanity did just as her mother said and didn't ask any more questions, she kept her mouth closed. As they walked up to the door, Catherine knocked four times. "Who is it," yelled a woman's voice. Catherine yelled back, "it's Catherine!" Catherine answered in a very seductive voice then the woman opened the door and hugged Catherine as tight as she could. "It's good to see you," Catherine said to the unknown woman.

"It's good to see you," the woman said. What took Sanity over the edge was when she heard Catherine say to the woman, "it's good to see you too mom," leaving Sanity even more confused as to why she was calling an unknown woman mom. "He's upstairs," the woman said to Catherine.

"Okay mom," she said back with a big bright smile on her face.

"Oh my God who is this beauty, is this your daughter Catherine," said the woman. She smiled and said, "Oh yes that's my beautiful daughter." For the first time Sanity heard her mom call her beautiful.

Chapter 7

It meant a lot to Sanity to be called beautiful by her mother. She was still puzzled as to why Catherine was there in the first place. However, she wasn't able to speak on it. The woman said, "baby you can have a seat on the couch right there," as Catherine began walking up the stairs to whoever she was going to see. Sanity sat on the couch in the living room of the woman's house with tears rolling down her cheeks. She wondered if Catherine was on drugs and is that why she acted like this. Every bad thought that could go through Sanity's head did. She just could not put two and two together and that frustrated her. The big and tall woman sat next to Sanity and asked, "are you okay baby, what's wrong, why are you crying, are you not comfortable, are you ready to go?"

"Yes, I'm ready to go, how long do you think my mom is going to be," Sanity said to the woman.

"Oh, baby you ready to go already normally when your mom comes over here, she be over here for a long time she probably should have just left you home baby so you can get some rest for school the next day."

"Oh, so she comes over here a lot," Sanity asked the woman.

"Well yes baby, her and my son are in love."

"Your son?" Sanity yelled, "well who is your son?" The woman's phone rang, she turned around, looked at Sanity, put her finger to her lips to quiet her and said, "hold on sweetheart I'll be right back." Before the woman could come back, Catherine came walking down the stairs with a very tall handsome man walking behind her. To Sanity's surprise it was Jimmy, the guy that TJ always had over to their house. The tears came even more. Sanity was in disbelief that her mom was seeing a friend of the family, so to say a man that actually spoke to her father every time he came over to their house. He would shake her father's hand every time he came to their house. *This can't be real* Sanity said to herself. Catherine gave Sanity a look like *you better not say nothing!* Jimmy walked over to Sanity smiling, "hey Sanity what's up how you doing girl?" Sanity could barely say anything. To please her mom and show her she would keep her mouth shut she said hi back to Jimmy. Jimmy then grabbed Sanity, "come here girl give me a hug. Stop acting like that, what's wrong with you?"

"Nothing, I'm just ready to go home," Sanity said. "I don't feel good," knowing that she was not telling the truth. She was wondering how her mother could put her in such a compromising situation knowing that Sanity had a lot of love for her dad regardless of how strict he was. She knew it was wrong.

Sanity did not look at Jimmy the same after that situation. She couldn't joke around with him anymore because it felt wrong. She felt violated in many ways because of the betrayal being done to her dad. "Sanity quit acting crazy girl," Catherine said. "What the hell is wrong with you?" She said it with an attitude as if Sanity was doing something wrong.

"Nothing," Sanity said, giving Catherine the same attitude because she knew what she was experiencing was not good. "I don't feel good I'm just ready to go my stomach hurt," Sanity said to Catherine, knowing that she wanted to run away and scream as loud as she could. She was just ready to get the hell out of there to face her family while carrying a horrible secret filled with lies and deceptions.

Days later when Jimmy came back over to Sanity's house, things felt very awkward. Sanity couldn't look Jimmy in the eyes. As time went on, it got worse for Sanity. Her name helped her survive after what she had to endure. If she had anything left it would have to have been her sanity. Of course, every time Jimmy came around, he tried to play with her a little more than ever in order to try to keep her on his good side and from telling what she knew about him and Catherine's secret relationship. Catherine started treating Sanity differently by showing her she really loved her, but deep down inside Sanity knew it was just a front so she would never open her mouth about what she had witnessed with her and Jimmy.

The same guy that came around the house often looked her father Willie in the eyes, shaking his hand, asking him how his days at work were, meanwhile the whole time sleeping with his woman. Sanity knew it was wrong but at the time it felt right just to get her mother's attention. She was willing to do anything just so her life would have felt right even if it meant betraying her father and living with the hurt and guilt for the rest of her life. That

was just the beginning for Sanity. The road got darker
and longer for this fifteen-year-old lost girl who
was trying to find a way out for her and her siblings.
Sanity felt as though Catherine knew it was wrong
and knew what mental damage it was doing to her,
but she didn't care. She was living in the moment of
what she called happiness and being free. Jimmy
preyed on the fact he already knew the dark secrets in
the house. He was there all the time with TJ, so he
already knew Catherine wasn't really happy with
Willie. He used that and Catherine didn't even see it
coming. She was so blinded by Jimmy's handsome
charming ways; she didn't care how it was affecting
her daughter.

Chapter 8

The taxi rides became more frequent, and Sanity was the chosen child to go with Catherine. Every time the taxi would come and pick them up no matter how bad it hurt Sanity, she still went just to please her mother and to get attention. Sanity noticed something was very off from everyone in the house. Every time she and her siblings would get into it, no one wanted to hear her side of the story. It was always "Sanity is lying," "you know Sanity is a liar," "don't believe nothing Sanity says." Sanity could not figure out why it felt like the whole family was against her all of a sudden. However, she didn't give it much thought, instead, she wrote more songs hoping one day she could get in the studio and sing or act, something that she had always dreamed of doing.

After laying across her grandmother's bed one day, Tim walked in through the side door. "Yo, Sanity! What you been doing all day sis," he asked. "Oh, nothing just resting," she said to Tim in a drowsy voice.

"Dang girl all you been doing is sleeping a lot lately what's wrong with you? Get up let's go on the porch and practice some songs together!"

"Okay Tim give me about ten more minutes," Sanity said. "I'm tired man."

"Sanity." Big Momma lightly tapped Sanity on what her grandmother would call a curvy booty. "Sanity get up you been sleeping all day girl! What's wrong with you? All you been doing is sleeping, your little butt better not be pregnant. You hear what I say girl? You can't take care of no damn baby right now and you know damn well your momma not doing it and I'm not raising no more babies."

"Big Momma what are you talking about?" Sanity said. "Ain't nobody pregnant because ain't nobody doing nothing Big Momma! I don't care nothing about no boys," Sanity said to her grandmother.

"Better not be I bet not hear nothing about you around those little boys," her grandmother said in a very demanding voice. Sanity got up because by that time she was so frustrated with her grandmother talking about her being pregnant and being around boys when she knew that was the last thing on her mind.

Sanity went outside on the porch with Tim. "What's up Tim," Sanity said. "My God I'm up now. Big Momma in there talking all crazy and stuff, talking about 'I bet not be pregnant' like who do she think I am?"

"Sis for real though you have been laying around a lot lately like something is wrong with you but Big Momma tripping you know how old people are. I don't know why she would think you're pregnant she knows you don't even be out here like that. Hell, Willie keeps us locked down all the time how and when you going to get pregnant?" He laughed out loud. "But no for real sis something wrong with you I can tell you been quiet and sleeping a lot lately you know you can talk to me. I mean I know you're older than me but I'm still here for you." Sanity started laughing with Tim.

"Boy shut up age ain't got nothing to do with it, but you know how our bond is right?" Tim looked at Sanity and smiled.

"Yeah, sis I know. But I'm not stupid I still know something is bothering you and you just don't want to say what it is. I'm going to wait on you to tell me whenever you get ready to so let's just leave that alone."

"I keep telling you ain't nothing wrong with me. I've just been tired lately that's it. I be up kind of late even when I'm laying down, I still be up looking at the wall just thinking about how we going to make it, that's all Tim."

"But anyway sis," Tim said, nudging her on the shoulder, "let's talk about this music thing. I know a dude named Triple O. I'm not sure yet but maybe he can let you come into the studio and do some music. I just got to check him out some more and see if it's a place that I need to be taking my sister around because you know how I am about you. I don't want to have to slap nobody about you," Tim laughed. It was something about Tim and his good spirit that he always found laughter in everything no matter how hard the times were or how bad he felt things were going for them in their home. He always laughed it off and always said he wasn't worried. He would say "stop worrying yourself things are going to get better for everybody."

Tim was holding a pen and notebook in his hand ready for Sanity to take control of what she was going to say but on paper. Tim looked at Sanity and said, "instead of worrying about it man, sis just write about it." Sanity snatched the pen and notebook from him and said, "you are always smiling about everything. You sure can take a lot because I can't take no more of this shit." She smiled right along with Tim. Tim had no idea Sanity was more so talking about the secret she had to keep quiet than the struggle, because the truth was in the small country town where they were from. A lot of families were struggling so it may have seemed like it was the normal way of living, but Sanity knew it had to have been a better way out. Sanity carried the guilt of hurting her father daily and no one saw that something was bothering her. In Sanity's household there was only one person that drove for many years and that was their granddad Marvin Jr. He worked a lot to also support the family's needs, so the children didn't get to see him much. For all of the store runs, the children would fight for whose turn it was to go, because for them that was also a peace of mind.

Chapter 9

Tim loved every bit of going to the store for everyone in the house so if one of the children didn't want to go Tim would be the first to yell "I'll go!" Of course, if Sanity didn't want to go, she jumped up running right behind her little brother. When the two of them got together all they talked about was their dreams of becoming rich and a way to make sure they followed their plans. Whatever Sanity had to do to talk about music and leaving the small town she did it so on every walk to the store with Tim was like a breath of fresh air she would start the conversation off with, "so what should we do first Tim?"

"You talked to Triple O today?"

"No!"

"How and we can't go nowhere today," Tim said with a stupid loud laugh. "Man let's just tell Willie we be going to the studio just to see what he say. He's not going to get mad when he finds out it's right around the corner." Triple O's inhouse studio sat across the street from another one of Sanity's family member's home and that was one of the houses Willie did not mind them playing at. However, they had to be home and in the house before the streetlights would come on. The kids knew this was one rule in their house that could never be broken, or they would be on restriction for months at a time. There were times Sanity and Tim broke many rules together without anyone ever knowing because Tim was so smart at getting away with things. Even if he felt he wouldn't get in trouble he still would and he was the only child brave enough to take a chance.

Although all of them were afraid of Willie's punishments, Tim still had the "I don't care" attitude at times. He felt like Willie was too hard on them as they watched a lot of their friends and other kids around the neighborhood do things they couldn't. Being young kids, they did not understand why he acted this way.

The kids missed out on a lot of things such as proper love because Catherine stayed in her own little world. Willie and Big Momma showed them as much love as they knew how to. Willie became angry and drank a lot. This became the norm for him, so of course, the home became an even more dysfunctional household. Willie had a big responsibility of helping Big Momma and grandpa, while keeping their house and children in order. Catherine should have made sure Willie at least had a good lunch for work each day, but she didn't. Willie would come home drunk, disturbing the whole household and then curse her out. Willie did this a lot in front of the kids and he didn't care who was there. The kids would cry and scream because they thought Willie was going to hit Catherine. Not once did he hit her, but she would scream to the top of her lungs scaring the kids even more.

For years the kids didn't understand why Willie drank so much. They loved their mom and dad very much and Sanity knew her mom never did anything to upset him so she couldn't understand why Willie treated Catherine as such. It was until one day after another long shameful day at school Sanity laid across the full-size bed her and her older sister Keisha shared with Big Momma. The house was silent. Sanity lifted her head up and said, "Big Momma where is everyone?" She looked back and said, "I don't know." Big Momma asked Sanity, "how the hell y'all can't keep up with each other but ya leave the house together and suppose to come home together?" Sanity gave her the biggest attitude because she knew nothing about sticking together in their house. "Girl you got any homework?" Big Momma yelled.

"Ma yes but I did it at school already," Sanity said.

"Gal you always say you already did it at school and your Momma don't give a damn. She don't never got time for her own damn kids with her slick ass."

Sanity sat up next to her grandmother on the bed and said, "where she at?"

"In her room somewhere looking in a mirror making sure she look good and y'all be running around here looking like who did it and why." That was one of Big Momma's favorite quotes for Sanity and her older sister Kiesha. Keisha was fed up with not being able to fit in with the other kids, so she learned how to do her own hair leaving Sanity to have to depend on Catherine to make sure she didn't get picked on in school for not having her hair done.

"Big Momma why you saying all of that?" Sanity asked while she was laughing. It was funny to her when she would hear her grandmother curse and get upset because she was always so nice to everyone. "Girl your momma full of shit," she said with her hand rested on her chin. "All she care about is herself. I know she better pay me back my money she owes me this Friday coming or it will be hell for her. She doesn't do nothing but borrow up my money to try to keep up with herself. It ain't like she is spending it on y'all. I'm behind now on my insurance bill she done had me get a loan on my life insurance fooling with her." Big Momma's forehead wrinkled.

"Ma why you keep giving it to her?" Sanity asked. "You see she taking forever to pay you back from the first time."

"I know. I hate I did it but she swear she gone give it all back on the first when she get that check she be getting for y'all."

Chapter 10

Sanity was so angry, but she did not show it. "What check did she get for us?" Sanity asked. "She don't give us no money!"

"I know, Big Momma said. "That's why your daddy be raising all that hell in here with her cause he give her all that money every week. That man be giving her his whole damn check for y'all and she still be borrowing up my money every chance she gets and don't tell nobody."

"Man, Ma I ain't going to lie that got me mad," Sanity said. "Because she don't be doing nothing for us maybe once a month she take us to that hair school downtown and let them girls burn our hair out with that stink hot straightening comb or she be telling them to give me and Keisha a reverse form of the jerry curl."

"That's what they call they self doing when y'all go there," Big Momma asked sarcastically.

"Yeah."

"So, they turn y'all jerry curl to a perm? She take y'all there because it's cheap. I just don't know for the life of me why that woman don't stop thinking she's going to be young forever and pay y'all some attention. Hell, she keep up with herself and y'all getting picked on in school? She ought to be ashamed of herself and she got everybody in the family and the streets talking about how she don't pay y'all no attention. Go in there and peep at her now. I guarantee she is in the mirror playing in her hair with a damn face full of makeup."

"Oh my God Momma! Why would you say that?" Sanity said with a chuckle in her voice.

Big Momma replied, "girl you will learn one day." She got her wooden pegs together to hang out two baskets of clothes she had spent all day hand washing in the bathtub. "Sanity come and help me get the dry clothes off of the clothesline and help me hang out y'all school clothes."

"Okay ma," Sanity said. She knew she couldn't say no even if she wanted to. Big Momma was what they called the heart of the house. She did everything for everyone inside and outside of their home. She had the warmest spirit and loved to sit at the edge of her bed while twisting her soft jet-black curly hair. She would wait until her favorite soap operas to come on which was her daily routine. Sanity had a pretty tight bond with Big Momma, and she learned everything from her. She followed her to the kitchen so she could watch her prepare big meals for the family. If it wasn't for Big Momma and Willie doing and providing as much as they could, Sanity and her siblings probably would have been put in Child Protective Custody.

Many days Sanity felt she probably would have been better off being stuck in a home with a mother that she didn't know at all rather than knowing Catherine was her mother. Catherine didn't have to tell the kids she hated being a mom because she showed it daily. It was as if she just wanted her own kids to disappear, but little did she know the feeling was mutual. Keisha and Joe knew how to hide their feelings well or they dealt with it by staying away from home as much as possible. There were eight adults in their home, and no one had a car except one person for many years. On top of this only two of them worked and that was Willie and their grandfather. A house full of family and they were the ones responsible for everyone that stayed there. Everyone had their own struggles however, it created arguments, and huge fights. Some family members would steal from one another to support their bad habits.

Tim was the child that made so many friends in the neighborhood, so it was easy for him to avoid the chaotic household filled with drama every single day even if it meant Willie putting him on punishment for long periods of times. Sanity spent most of her time writing songs that would match her pain and fears of making it out of the hood with a strong mindset to build a better life for her own future. She always felt better after she wrote her feelings on paper even if she wrote about it and tore it up. It gave her confirmation that she would be able to get through life's challenges. There were many family issues Sanity escaped from but one of her main ways of running from it was to watch television shows that had anything to do with singing and talk show hosting. Sanity and Big Momma would be ready for the show called *Star Search* and *Show Time at the Apollo*. They did their best not to miss a single show. The funny thing is, no matter what was going on around them, they had a way of tuning it out without a problem while the shows were on. Big Momma knew Sanity loved music so she just kind of got sucked into it by sitting with Sanity watching her favorite talent shows with her. There were only a few places the kids were allowed to watch TV. Big Momma's room was one of the main places because the house was so crowded. The kids' best choice was to sit in Big Momma's room. She didn't mind and this is how Sanity won Big Momma over. They listened to music as well but one thing she always said was "girl that ain't no real music the most beautiful music is Opera!"

Sanity laughed so hard and said, "Ma wait! Don't nobody our age listen to that and besides our choir teacher be making us sing that kind of music."

Chapter 11

Big Momma looked over at Sanity and said, "girl hush you don't know real good music!"

Then comes Tim walking in the room yelling out his favorite saying, "who dat," as loud as he could making Big Momma curse again so they could laugh. Tim knew the louder he was, the more it would make her stare at them. The look is what they looked forward to seeing from her because it was the funniest thing ever to them.

"Tim where you been boy?" Big Momma asked. He told her he was at his friend's house. She looked at him and said, "boy you ain't never at home you are running the streets like you're grown!"

Tim said jokingly, "the streets are my home Big Momma." Not knowing that Tim really felt that way. No matter how much Big Momma and their dad tried to make sure all of the younger kids were comfortable it didn't seem to work out that way. Tim's resting place in the house was wherever he could lay. Most of the time that was stretched out across Big Momma's floor with a sheet thrown over him for comfort. Not one time had Tim complained to anyone in the house. He only expressed how he truly felt to Sanity and he would include Big Momma in the conversation at times because all of the kids knew their secrets were safe with her. They believed they wouldn't be in trouble for saying how they truly felt to Big Momma. All of the other adults in the house would say, "you ain't grown it don't matter how you feel, you're a child." That was one of the things that got under Sanity's skin badly because in her mind she was already in the battlefield with the secret she was holding to protect her mother, Catherine. She was never worried about her dad physically abusing her mom because he never laid a hand on her. She was worried the blame would be on her for not saying something sooner and it would cause her mom not to love her again.

Sanity was tricked into believing that she must be submissive to Catherine in order to get the love and attention that she truly desired. She felt the love from everyone else naturally, but it came with a price when it came to Catherine. Sanity was okay with getting love from Catherine rather it being fake or real, the feeling was different and felt so real. In the moment, Sanity's biggest prayer was "Lord don't let me be the one to tell the secret." She hoped someone else who knew about it would tell it and that would have kept her in the clear. Not knowing either way if it had gotten out, she still would have been blamed for not saying anything to anyone especially Tim. She knew if she told Tim, it would have taken a turn for the worse because Tim was crazy about Willie and they had an unbreakable bond. The last thing Sanity wanted to do was hurt their dad in any way. They knew Willie was big on loyalty and he would raise all kinds of hell, as the good old folks would say. Sanity felt that if she didn't say anything about Catherine's horrible secret their life would have been better off and the only person that would be damaged or hurt would be her.

It became the norm because it got easier to deal with for Sanity as time went by. The scars remain and she knew part of it would have been a lifetime of pain for her. Not thinking if she ever thought about having children, it would also cause damage to them as well especially a little girl. Mentally things got worse for Sanity and the only person who noticed was one of Sanity's best friends, her little brother Tim. What made it hard for him was he saw the change in Santy's behavior; however, he had no clue what was causing the change in his sister. He asked her many times what was going on with her and she always told him nothing or would catch an attitude with him for asking so he just stopped. He went on assuming that when she was ready, she would tell him. If no one else knew he knew one day Sanity would sit down with him and tell him everything on her mind.

Sanity was broken in a million pieces and no matter how loud she cried out no one in their house noticed it but Tim. He was working on trying to get it out of her, but it was the hardest thing to do because of her loyalty to Catherine. Sanity carried the weight for a while. She made it unrecognizable to the outside world. Plus, she knew how to wear the best on the outside because if Catherine didn't teach her anything else she made sure she knew how to cover up dishonesty and how to throw her loyalty for Willie right out the window. This left a broken heart full of scars and Sanity always wondered if the scars would ever heal. After sitting in the room with Big Momma, Tim asked Sanity to walk to the neighborhood corner store one day before Willie got in from another long day at the cotton plant. Willie worked this job since

Sanity was a toddler. His job was more than just a job to him, it was a family away from home. Willie's boss loved everyone in their household because they were so familiar with all of his kids coming to see him on his lunch breaks or at the job site to get their weekly allowance outside of what he gave Catherine weekly for them. Three to five dollars wasn't much for some, but to them it was a lot. One thing Willie did not play about, he always made sure the kids felt loved and their weekly allowance was just another way of showing them this. Their daddy truly was doing everything he could to make sure they had everything they needed and some. Poor Willie had a lot on his plate with helping Big Momma and Grandpa with all of the bills and raising children that required a lot because they were all school age.

Chapter 12

Big Momma made raising the kids look so easy, especially the girls. Anytime Sanity or Keisha went to her for anything, if she didn't have it, she would go an extra mile to try and get what her girls needed. She didn't care about calling up her long-time personal insurance agent to borrow money off of her policy when it came to them. Big Momma was one of the most powerful loving women in the small little country town. Of course, Willie and Catherine's kids got more attention from Big Momma then her other grandchildren outside of the home. For years Sanity wanted to tell her cousins that Big Momma didn't care or love them anymore than she did any of her grandchildren and she was forced to step in to help Willie raise them. She stepped in for them because she saw firsthand what life would have been like for them without her. Big Momma always said, "it took a village to raise a family" and she was so good at helping raise the children. That woman had all of the old-time home remedies for everything and everyone. That's why she was like a superhero to Sanity. In Sanity's heart she felt as if Big Momma was the next best thing to God and that's how Sanity saw her.

There wasn't anything Big Momma didn't have the answers to whenever Sanity or Keisha asked. No matter what she was doing around the house she tried her best to include them even when she had to do something for her husband. She would call the girls and her favorite words would be, "you see here y'all?" That's when they knew it was another lesson to be learned by their superwoman. While she would teach, she usually would have a powerful speech to go with it explaining to them what it took to be a great wife to their husbands someday if they had ever considered getting married. Sanity listened in on conversations she shouldn't have and in doing so she also learned their Grandfather had some infidelity throughout a period of their marriage. He fathered several other children with several other women, but Sanity and her siblings had never seen them. Big Momma said it loud and clear that his out-side children were not allowed anywhere near the family without her knowledge. So, they never spoke on it in their house as everyone knew it was a sensitive subject for Big Momma.

Sanity was afraid there would be rumors of her knowledge of the infidelities occurring between Catherine and their father. Sanity was taught betrayal at a very tender age and she did not agree with it. However, she started to believe that you had to do what you had to do to get what you wanted. As time passed Sanity looked at her friend's hair and asked them questions about how they would do their hair. She started learning little by little so that she could try to do her own hair without bothering anyone and it didn't turn out too well. She couldn't get the hair idea together right then. Sanity became more of a tomboy because most of her friends were, however, they kept their hair really pretty. One of the great things about Sanity's friends was they did not pick on her because her hair wasn't done properly. They saw her for who she really was and that was their good friend including her male friends. Sanity's outgoing and outspoken spirit helped her gain a lot of friends and they didn't see her for nothing or no one other than their friend.

Sanity got to a point where she knew she needed to learn how to make herself look beautiful without having to pay the price. It wasn't until a few years passed that she was able to get her hair situation together which stopped people from bullying her. By the time Sanity received compliments and attention she started to lose patience for doing the right things.

She felt as if things were feeling different inside and out. The only thing is she could not figure out what the new feeling was. It didn't feel good, and it didn't feel bad. It just wasn't a normal feeling to her. She knew she needed to press the gas and come up with a plan to get away from her pain even if it meant stepping outside of who she really was. Sanity's dreams were so much bigger than her hometown living situation and rather she chose it, or it was the hand she was dealt. One thing Sanity had to remember was you have to play to win with the hand you're dealt. Tim had that "I don't give a damn" attitude and this attitude said, "we will make it out of this town, and we will do it big too." Tim's attitude gave Sanity all the hope she needed to be the best she could be and at least make her father and Grandparents proud. She wanted to show them how much she appreciated their effort with raising her and her siblings. It wasn't that Sanity did not want to give their mother props for her part in raising them, but her part was damaging. Sanity often wondered if

Catherine even cared or saw how much her absence weighed on them. Yes of course, Catherine was physically there, but she was absent emotionally and mentally for Sanity. Every time Sanity asked for help with schoolwork, Catherine told her and the others the same thing, "didn't y'all asses pay attention in school where the hell are your notes?"

Their response every time was, "okay Catherine never mind." They would get up and walk away feeling angrier each time. They just gave up on asking for help and started figuring things out on their own because they knew Willie was already giving all he had.

Chapter 13

Even though Catherine was present in the home, the emotional and mental part of her being in the kid's life was a dead end. It was either her not knowing or her just not caring at all but that was something the children never understood. As time passed by, they accepted it for what it was, Tim especially. Sanity was the one that no matter what she felt she needed to and wanted to fight a little harder and longer for Catherine's love and attention. This was even if she had to withhold such an unbelievable secret. Sanity believed showing their mother loyalty would have been better because none of the other children would have done it for her. They all loved Willie to death. Sanity trusted and loved Willie with her whole heart because he made sure he was never absent in none of their lives. He was overly strict, but they felt every ounce of the love Willie had to give. He was their superman no matter how much hell he raised. It was easy for them to overlook a lot of it because they knew that Willie was dealing with the weight of trying to be the best father he could be while trying to make sure Big Momma and their Grandpa was always straight because they were getting older.

One thing Catherine did do was care for her father when he had his days of not feeling so well, but that wasn't that often. Catherine somehow felt as if caring for her dad was the number one thing in her life even over her children, but everyone had that all figured out. Catherine knew her dad saw no wrong in her, so she made sure she kept that bond with him.

Not knowing she was putting up a great front to her own children causing them to lose themselves in the midst of it all.

One day after a long walk to the other side of town, Sanity expressed to Tim how lost she felt in life. She kept asking him if the music didn't take off what would be the next step. Sanity always thought of the next best move in case no one would take them seriously because of their ages. The lack of support made it hard for them to chase their dreams. As the conversation carried on, Sanity still felt empty and lost inside. She said to Tim, "man forget this we need to go to the studio today and make a song so that I can send it to *Show Time at the Apollo*."

She knew even if she were selected Willie was not having his little girl catching a flight to New York City to compete in a competition. It wasn't because Willie didn't support her music, he thought she was too young and of course he was very overprotective. Willie wasn't like that with just her, he treated all of his children the same. He was a man that stood by everything he said and when he said he will do any and everything in the world to protect them he meant it. Although Willie fussed every day, they felt protected and loved. The only thing missing was that Catherine didn't show the same love Willie showed.

Sanity often wondered why Catherine was silent about everything that would happen or take place in their lives. Catherine would give off weird vibes whenever they would need her to be there for them. It weighed heavily on Sanity, but she dealt with the pain the best way she knew how. Sanity always wanted what was best for her siblings even if it meant removing herself from the equation. Tim felt the same way and Sanity knew because of the many conversations they had over the years. As they were walking down the long-paved road the conversation became deeper and deeper. Tim asked Sanity, "man sis why do you think Willie be arguing so much?"

Sanity said, "think about it bro. He does everything with the help of Big Momma by himself. I probably would be mad too. I mean I don't know. You see every time we go to Catherine for anything, she tells us to go to him. I'm not going to lie, sometimes I be scared to go to him because we go to him so much. If not him then we have to go to Big Momma. Of course, Big Momma will have to go to grandpa." Tim agreed with Sanity. Their grandfather was a great man like Willie. They believed in true family values by providing and showing the children skills they needed throughout life. Tim replied to Sanity, "yeah man I feel the same way that's why I asked you that question. I thought I was tripping though." He shook his head slowly.

Sanity said, "I ain't saying she don't love us but dang she doesn't show us like our daddy does. It's like every time we go to her about anything, she gets a horrible attitude with us. It makes you scared to even ask for something. Come on now Tim you act like that's not the truth. I done seen you come from her door looking all sad like a puppy because she yelled out one of her nasty curse words again."

Tim laughed, "girl you crazy. She does that all the time. I be wanting to ask her what are you screaming for? But for real it don't bother me. When she do that I'm so used to it now shoot she do it all the time. We just got to go to the studio and make some music so we can get a record deal and move all of us away."

Chapter 14

Tim thought if they moved to another state Catherine would act different towards them. Sanity kept her feelings to herself when Tim would talk about relocating to another state. Sanity and Tim's agenda was the same to a certain extent. Sanity knew relocating wouldn't change Catherine's ways, but Tim thought the opposite. Tim's exact words were "I can't wait until we move so Catherine can act normal. She doesn't act like our other friends' mommas. They play with their kids and go places like a family. They even sit at the dinner table together and we don't never do that."

Sanity did not want to crush Tim's feelings and hopes that things would change with going away from all of their family. The times Catherine did mix and mingle with the family she would say "don't y'all be taking no news out of this house!" This meant all of the kids knew not to tell anyone anything that didn't live in their house. Somehow certain things would be talked about between some of their family members. Big Momma would call it venting and sometimes when her other children would come over to visit her, she would talk about things on her mind.

Big Momma had a way with spilling the beans to everyone. No one was safe so if anyone did anything or she ever heard any of the family was into something, she didn't have a problem with sharing the news. If anyone wanted to confront her well, she was fine with that too. All she would say is, "you're damn right I said it!" She was very blunt, and this is another reason why the family loved her. The only problem was many of the family's generations were ruined early on by dishonesty and trustworthiness. The lessons were passed on from generations to generations, and so many of the older people had to learn as they go. They figured it out on their own and did the best they could. For those families, it was taken as a blessing to have had a family member that was wise enough to realize what some of the most important values of family were. Big Momma fits the category for world best Momma.

Tim held it together way better than Sanity did. All of her siblings seemed a bit stronger than her. Sanity probably felt that way because she spent her alone time constantly reminding herself of wanting to grow up fast enough to be able to repay Big Momma, their grandpa, and Willie for everything. Sanity's hopes and dreams were that everything would turn around in her favor and fairness in their home. She always felt like she and Tim were treated differently from their brothers and sisters. Sanity's hopes were that somewhere underneath all of the hurt the answers would be found.

Sanity was ambitious. If she wanted to figure something out or needed answers to any of her questions she wouldn't stop until it was fulfilled by any means necessary. When Tim and Sanity would have their little one on one talks, he already knew that Sanity said she was going to do something no matter if it was right or wrong. Tim knew Sanity would make a way to get it done. She said she was going to leave the small country town once she got older and this was something she really wanted to do.

Tim's agenda was different from Sanity's. Tim had in his mind when he and Sanity made a way out, the whole family would be on a path to another way of living. Since Sanity was a little older than Tim, she knew better. Sanity sat around listening and grasping the issues their family had. She realized there were too many problems to relocate to another state or even another city. Moving wouldn't fix the problems within the family. The kids spent a lot of time watching family movies with Big Momma and the movies would portray families moving away to start over. Tim didn't separate the fact that these were movies and reality. It takes more than just packing up and moving away. Sanity knew doing this would come along with the same secrets and problems and moving them away with her would have only made things worse. She always knew if they were going to move then it needed to be done the right way. There would have to be no regrets when they both leave. They would have to make sure this is what the family needed. They would have to get everything in order first.

Chapter 15

Sanity knew the older family members in the house were already set in their ways. Their minds were already made up with the lifestyle they were living. Sanity did not hold that against them because they had already lived most of their best years enjoying life as it was. In Sanity's mind, she and her siblings had such a bright future ahead of them because they were still young, and their dreams were still fresh. Sanity and Tim's walks took longer than expected but that wasn't the first time they walked until dark fell. One of Willie's rules was not to let the streetlights catch them and all of the kids knew that was just another way of Willie being a father. Willie wanted to protect them from any and everything that moved. He stayed on edge everyday thinking that being so hard on them would have kept all of the kids out of harm's way and turn them into angels. People in the community knew Willie for being the overprotective father. They never would say or approach him about anything. Willie's intentions were never to intimidate anyone, it was simply to let the world know that he did not play about his kids. In his eyes, it did not matter if they were right or wrong.

After reminiscing about relocating for over thirty minutes, Sanity and Tim's conversation led them straight to the studio. Tim felt as if it was already dark, they were already in trouble, so if they were going to get spanked or put on punishment it should have counted for something good like making music in the studio. Sanity felt in her heart that Tim was also treated differently by Catherine and it seemed as if they both were suffering in different ways. Tim knew how to put the best look on the outside. Even though Tim was younger than her, she watched his strength and learned how to cover up her pain. She would put a bandage on every wound day by day and low and behold, the girl had it all figured out. In her mind she would say, *if I act like I don't hurt then the hurting would stop.* It seemed as if the more Catherine saw how hurt Sanity was, the more she would contribute to the pain. For years Sanity didn't want to deal with this. As time went on, if anything would happen around the house, Catherine would blame Sanity or Tim. They were never recognized when anything good happened around the house. Catherine painted this misleading picture about Sanity and Tim.

Sanity and her cousin grew up very close to one another. Whenever they would come over to visit, they all would come up with a plan for them to get out of their situations. Their situations were small compared to what Sanity was going through. The three cousins Sanity was close with would fake like they were crying so that Sanity and Keisha could spend at least one night with them. Sanity and Keisha's cousins had it all figured out before they would come over, but sadly Sanity and Keisha would be told they couldn't go. When Sanity cried, her tears were so real because some of the best days were spent with her cousins given the fact that no one knew what Sanity went through and how she truly felt inside. It was easier keeping it to herself because she felt her voice was already taken away by Catherine and her own lies. Sometimes Sanity would cry so hard that Willie would give in and let her go with her cousins. Willie would always have a long talk with the adult that was responsible for his precious little girls no matter how old his daughters were they will always be his little girls. Every time he would say, "don't let shit happen to my babies, you hear me?"

Willie didn't care how much he screamed at anyone when it came to his kids and if they changed their mind, he would flip out. He would have assumed everyone thought their kids were better than his and Willie would have fought hard about that. Willie made it known that he would die and go to hell for all of his kids. Even when he was intoxicated his words never changed and that was just another reason Sanity didn't look at Willie any different. Sanity had more than a few reasons to look at their dad different than the rest of her siblings.

Chapter 16

Sanity saw more good than bad in their dad. Yes, he drank a little more than he should have, and yes, he fussed and cursed a lot. This allowed Catherine to have the advantage to tell the entire family and outside how horrible he was even when it came to the way he treated the kids. In Sanity's eyes, she felt it was fair to say Willie wasn't all wrong. He was dealing with the weight of the world on his shoulders and the burden of having to take care of the entire household. Sanity kind of understood Willie and why he was emotionally abusive toward Catherine. Not to say that it was the right thing to do but Big Momma always said, "even a dog gets tired."

All of the kids had their chance of sitting around while family was over listening to Catherine tell her side of the story about Willie and his "crazy deranged ways," what she would call it. The sad truth is Sanity spent a lot of nights crying for God to heal Catherine's soul because it was so evil and broken for whatever reasons. Catherine seemed to never care about her kids so the fight for Sanity was endless. Sanity knew how to pray because her other grandmother, who was Willie's mother. She had taught her who God really was at a very young age as she spent most of her toddler years with that side of the family. Church was always their first priority in their family home. This was where she picked up her singing voice from. However, this was added to her list of things being overlooked because no one took her seriously other than Tim.

Wanting to step out into the world of music wasn't heard of or talked about in their hometown because everybody was too busy trying to make a better way for themselves. Sanity loved music so much that no matter what anyone else said about it mattered. Sanity had a cousin on her dad's side that loved music as well. The two of them were inseparable when it came to remaking real artist's music. When the two of them got together that's all they did was sing until they got on everyone's nerves in the house. Sanity would think it was a good idea to sing loudly so everyone could hear them. They would get fussed at whenever they did this. The two cousins thought it was so funny when their sweet little grandmother would simply come to the door and say, "Sanity baby can y'all lower your voice?" This grandmother was another one of the world's best grandmother to all of her grandchildren, rather they spent a lot of time with her or not. She showed them genuine love all the time and they would feel the love in her hugs and sweet kisses on their cheeks. After she would grab a chair to sit and listen to them sing and then all four of Sanity's Aunts would come in and have a seat as if they were performing for them. This is what Sanity loved about her Aunts on her dad's side.

Her dad's side of the family made sure no matter what any of the kids in the family were into, they tried their best to be there for them. Not that Catherine's siblings weren't there for them, but it was the fact that it really didn't matter to Catherine what the kids had going on in their lives. Their grandpa and Willie were always working leaving Big Momma to be there for the kids as much as she could. With her age being a problem, Big Momma taught the kids everything she could to be a survivalist; some took notes, and some didn't.

Catherine's sisters and brothers didn't have a clue what her kids were into when it came to school and hobbies. Catherine never expressed her kids' interest to anyone because she didn't really know what her kid's dreams were. She heard Sanity singing, Tim rapping, and Joe knee deep into sports meanwhile Keisha never spoke on much of anything. Keisha is the oldest, so her feelings were already going numb toward the entire situation. Singing and acting was personal for Sanity because the studio was a place she could express her feelings. She figured if she had ever gotten a shot at acting or singing it would finally ease all of her pain.

Sanity heard of a magnificent guy that did some of the funniest stage plays by the name of Tyler Perry. She tried everything she could to have a shot with Tyler Perry. She sent emails and called every number posted online that would have connected her to him. She even mailed out multiple letters to all of the addresses she found online for his establishment. Not only did she do everything she could to reach him she also emailed and mailed letters to Oprah Winfrey, Jenny Jones, Ricky Lake and any talk show host popular at the time. She was dedicated to landing her acting career. Whenever she would help someone else, it would give her the motivation to keep pushing in hopes of her own dreams.

The very first time Sanity saw one of Tyler Perry's shows, something shifted in her spirit. She thought to herself this was exactly what her passion was, and it would have been the best thing to have happened to her. Watching how passionate he was about his work and everyone on his team got Sanity excited about singing and acting. Whenever he would speak at the end of his plays, she would feel as if the messages he delivered were directly for her. If she had spoken on it everyone would have thought she was crazy.

Chapter 17

Sanity had put in her head that all she really needed to do was relocate to Atlanta because she heard that is where Tyler Perry was located. She knew if she could get near him for one conversation it would have made a difference in her life even if she didn't get a chance to work with him. She knew his uplifting encouraging words would have made her life feel so much more worth it. Sanity wanted to write plays as well, but the sad part was if she had ever got a chance to do this all of her plays would be on everything she was experiencing mentally and emotionally. Most of her scenes would show mothers going against their daughters and the tragedy that could come with it.

The next day Tim asked Sanity if she wanted to help him clean a neighbor's yard because it was something they did on the weekends for extra money.

"Yes, I will go," she said back in a slow sleepy voice. After that they decided to go to the studio. She just couldn't turn Tim down. As the two got further down the street near Triple O's place, Tim yelled out, "ayyyoo!" Triple O knew it was them. Whenever Sanity and Tim would go to record some music, he would get excited. He loved hearing Sanity pour her heart out through the mic. Whenever Tim would take over, he would jump up and down yelling "yo yo that shit is so dope!" Triple O had always told them that they were what the city was missing and that really stuck with Sanity. That was all she thought about day and night. Tim told Triple O to stop the music so that he could get a drink of water before recording another track, even though the music was muted.

The energy in the room was high. They all were laughing and having a good time. It was almost like a party was going on. Then Triple O said, "naw for real Sanity you need to go ahead and let me really record you like make an album and do a photo shoot and all. We can burn some CD's and sell some and send some to different recording labels and see who will sign you." He gave Sanity so much hope in her dreams and that is what kept Sanity and Tim going to the studio every single day. Tim and Sanity had it so bad they would break curfew a few times a week knowing that there would be consequences that they would have to face with Willie. The punishments would have been longer as time went on but that did not phase them because they felt like it was for a good cause. Tim felt it would have given them just what their family needed because this would have jump-started them to a new location and life. Sanity said to Triple O, "are you serious you know my dad will not let me do all of that." She shook her head slowly from side to side as her eyes filled with tears.

She became so emotional every time she was reminded, she really could do this. Out of all of the thoughts that were going through her head the number one thing that bothered her the most was that her little brother had so much hope and faith in her and the last thing she wanted to do was disappoint him. It was now or never for Sanity and she was willing to do whatever it took to make Tim's dreams come true. He was the main one supporting her throughout it all.

Sanity got up every day with music on her mind because she loved it. She saw how every time she sang it blew Tim's mind and it motivated her even more. As they were getting ready to leave the studio, Tim went ahead and finished talking for Sanity on her behalf because he knew that she would have been too scared to ask Willie if it was okay to work with Triple O. He said to Triple O, "okay O let us know when you want use to come for the photos and whatever else we need to do."

"Okay I will brother," Triple O replied. "And Sanity loosen up, it'll be okay." He smiled at Sanity and said, "Girl You better get with the program it's money to be made and it's up to you if you want it or not." Sanity thought about all of that but still was too afraid to let Willie know that she wanted to live out her dream at such a young age. As Tim and Sanity walked down the stairs leaving the studio, Tim stopped Sanity by grabbing her by her arm and said, "sis you need to really calm down it's not that serious and we won't know unless we ask him. Maybe Willie will say yeah. He knows how much you like music right?"

Sanity shook her head up and down and replied, "yes" very softly. Sanity's problem was she was always afraid to open up because no one would believe in her dreams like herself. She kept that between her and Tim. Everybody in Sanity's entire family knew that she would walk around the house singing or listening to music all the time, but they didn't know she actually wanted to become a singer or actor. No one ever asked her or sat her down to try to figure out what she wanted to do with her life.

Sanity and Big Momma were so close she expressed how she felt with Big Momma a lot. Big Momma was one of the only other people who knew what her dreams were, and she showed as much interest as she could. However, Sanity kept in mind that Big Momma's hands were full because she was trying to run a whole houseful of children and grown adults. Big Momma had to look after the adults in the house too because some were doing their own things, staying out late at night, and getting into trouble in the streets. When they would come home, they would have disagreements trying to fight each other and Big Momma would always have to be the one to get in between them and make sure that they didn't kill each other. For some reason, Sanity did not hold that against her. She knew Big Momma was there as much as she could be for her because she knew Big Momma had to also watch after her other siblings as well. Whenever Sanity sat and told Big Momma what she wanted to do Big Momma always would show a lot of interest in it; however, it wasn't much she could have done and that alone meant the world to Sanity.

Chapter 18

Whenever Big Momma would watch shows that had singing or dancing in it, she would call Sanity to let her know to come watch it with her. This is something Sanity never forgot, and it kept a very warm spot in Sanity's heart for her. Sanity was one of those young girls that had dreams so big, if she told people what she wanted to do and what her goals were, it would probably have been a joke to many people. In the small town they grew up in not many people came forward and said what they actually wanted to do with their lives. Sanity wanted to be one of the world's biggest stars. Sanity looked at music differently. She wanted to sing music that would heal broken hearts, give closure to painful situations, and fix people's crown. Sanity was all for it.

Sanity would listen to certain songs she could relate to and it would always make her feel like a weight was lifted off her shoulders even if it was just for a little while. She would feel in the end the song was worth listening to. Sanity also felt that Willie knew how much she loved music and he wanted her to make it, however he just felt that the timing was wrong given the fact that she was so young, and he was so overprotective. He felt if he had let her go that would have been the end of her.

Sanity going in the studio and being there all night without Willie's permission would have been the absolute biggest punishment she had ever gotten. This is why every trip to the studio was between her and Tim. No one else knew about it because she and Tim knew how to keep secrets together. The only thing that was still eating Sanity's heart alive was the fact that she was going through so much mentally and emotionally due to what Catherine had exposed her to and Tim still knew nothing about it. They had always had this bond and they didn't keep anything from each other but that was just one thing that Sanity felt she could never tell him because he would have flipped then the secret would have gotten out. Sanity would then put all of the blame on herself as she had already done for everything else. This is something Sanity only knew how to do. She blamed herself for any and everything that went wrong because this is how she grew up and was raised.

Catherine's and Sanity relationship was so toxic the only thing is no one in the house could see it but Sanity definitely did. Tim saw bits and pieces and he would mention certain things to Sanity, but he wouldn't say much. Tim always wanted everything to be perfect in their family and Sanity did too. She was sure all of her siblings wanted everything to be perfect but the one thing that was missing was the fact that they were not taught how to love each other. They were taught how to be divided. Willie, Big Momma, and their grandfather didn't teach them how to be divided; it was all of Catherine's doing. They hardly ever had conversations with the other adults in the house, so they didn't teach them either.
Through all of Catherine's actions it showed them that love wasn't important, trust wasn't important, and being dishonest was at the top of the list in their household.

Sanity thought to herself many days if she could have just told Tim what was bothering her for so long and he would have just taken it easy and not mentioned anything about it to anyone. She would have felt so much better because he was her comfort zone, and she knew that telling him would have also lifted a weight off of her shoulder. Sanity thought about what the outcome would have been if she had said anything. She wondered if Tim would have looked at her differently or if Willie would have hated her. She wondered if anyone would have believed her. After all, Catherine saw nothing wrong with painting the horrible picture that Sanity was such a liar and had already told many family members never to believe anything she said.

Catherine didn't understand how much damage she had done to Sanity. What she did was take Sanity's voice away before she would even know how to speak. This kept Sanity from opening up about a lot of things to people when certain incidents would take place. For example, whenever she would get bullied or picked on in school, she didn't know how to let the teachers know or tell the principal. In her mind since everyone in her house had already deemed her as a liar, because of Catherine's ironic stories, she figured no one would ever believe her. Sanity felt there was no need in her even speaking up for herself. She also began to look at everyone different, even the few friends that she had at school. Her trust level for people was very low because all of the trust she had put in her mom was just thrown away. All it took was a few trips to an old

rundown apartment complex and to the level 1A
camp prison yard. The prisoners had more freedom
than any other prisoners. Sanity was just a little girl at
the time of these specific visits. Catherine made her
keep an eye out for the guards while she had sex
across from the picnic table Sanity was sitting at.
This scarred Sanity.

The run-down complex was where Catherine
took Sanity frequently to sit with her as a cover up to
see her lover Jimmie, where he lived with his mother.
He went to prison because he got caught up in the
streets doing robberies and drugs. Sanity wondered
why Catherine would always cut holes in her pants
during visitation days. She found out she would do
this to please Jimmie out on the yard during visitation
hours. Sanity had to watch out for the prison guards
to make sure that Catherine and Jimmie didn't get
caught having sex, but it got worse. She was told by
Catherine to watch out for other couples in the
visitation area once they were done. Sanity felt
disgusted, used and abused. Sanity did everything she
could to just keep her head down and not look up at
them and that's when she made the biggest mistake
and looked up and she looked at Jimmie and he was
stroking Catherine and staring at her at the same time
with the most perverted look on his face as he bit his
bottom lip making light moans.

Chapter 19

Willie would tell Catherine he loved her every morning before he left for work and Catherine's reply was, "I love you too see you when you get off." If Catherine only knew how much Sanity really looked up to her and really wanted to be just like her. All she saw was a powerful beautiful woman but behind all of the makeup, nice clothes, and beautiful hair. What she saw didn't even matter anymore because the actions were totally different. Catherine didn't see Sanity for that and as a matter-of-fact Catherine saw none of her kids for nothing more than just kids. Anytime the kids needed or wanted anything they knew exactly who to go to, Big Momma, Willie or their Grandfather.

When the rest of the family would come over to visit there were times that some of them would question it and say "damn y'all ask Big Momma for everything! Why didn't you go around there and ask your mom for it?" It was embarrassing for Sanity and her siblings, but she never approached them about it because she knew that deep down inside, they all had different feelings towards Catherine. Sanity had her worries about her little sister growing up and possibly feeling the same way she felt towards Catherine but despite how she felt towards Catherine she didn't want her other siblings to feel the way she felt. It wasn't a good feeling at all and probably one of the most horrible feelings a child could have.

Sanity kept all of her feelings and emotions bottled up inside. She felt that if she had given Tim any clue of what was going on it would have just given him mixed emotions and caused him to hate Catherine. Everyone knew Tim and Willie had a bond that nothing or no one could have ever destroyed. Tim was Willie's closest child. Tim was the youngest and he spent more time with Willie than the rest of his siblings. The only reason why the other children didn't hang out as much as Tim did with him was because they were all too busy trying to figure out life. One thing everyone knew about Willie was that he never put any of his kids before the other. He truly believed in showing and giving them an equal amount of love. However, all of the kids were still very much confused with Catherine's actions and the way that she showed love to them. Sanity felt that Catherine thought that it was okay to not show her kids any type of love or emotions. This turned Sanity's life in many different directions.

Catherine couldn't see past her own selfishness and greed. Catherine didn't see past her nice hair dos and full faced makeup. She was so standoff with the kids even when it came to teaching the girls the things that they needed to learn. Big Momma had to step up to the plate to teach them as they got older. All of the kids knew that it was hard on Big Momma, but they also knew that Big Momma was there for whatever they needed. One thing about Big Momma was she never complained about doing anything for anyone. There were times they would hear her say, "Lord I'm so tired." Sanity and Keisha would ask her was she okay and of course she would reply, "yeah I'm okay. I'm just sleepy."

Deep down inside the girls knew Big Momma was actually tired of being there and tried to stay so strong for everyone. Her powerful soul wouldn't let her quit being so helpful and loving. It was her best trait, something that Catherine clearly didn't inherit. Sanity oftentimes questioned herself and her existence. She wondered why Catherine hates her so much and if everything was her fault. She thought maybe if she wasn't here Catherine would be much happier. Catherine would yell or curse at Sanity and say, "you act just like your damn daddy." She was often blamed for something she truly didn't do and if she tried to explain herself or say it wasn't her, Catherine would automatically shut her down. Catherine would tell her she is simple minded. However, Sanity noticed Catherine would never say any of that in front of Willie.

Sanity started to believe the only reason she was looked over and talked down to so bad was because Catherine really hated Willie inside and whenever she looked at Sanity, it was just like looking at him. Sanity resembled Willie. The feelings Catherine had towards him were toxic as well, so Sanity was feeling every bit of hatred she had towards Willie. She woke up every day with the feeling that Catherine hated all of them. As time went by Sanity wanted to stay away from the house more and more. Every day she tried to come up with a plan so that she could have gone missing from the drama. She couldn't wait for her cousins to come over and visit so that they could come up with a plan for her and Keisha to leave with them for a weekend.

Chapter 20

Sanity and Keisha didn't have to rehearse getting their way. They usually would have it planned out because it was routine. None of the adults knew what they were up to which made them laugh. Sanity and Keshia loved being around family. When they would leave home for the weekend with their cousins, they were able to see how loving families appreciate one another. This gave them the hope they needed that loving families do exist. Whenever Sanity and Keisha would go spend the weekends with their cousins, they would always hear their aunts and uncles tell their kids that they love them. Their aunts and uncles made sure Sanity and Keisha felt loved too.

Whenever it was time for bed, their aunts and uncles would give them a goodnight kiss. Sanity and Keisha were well behaved when they went over to their cousin's house. Their aunts and uncles didn't mind whenever they would want to come over and spend the night. Not sure if they knew it was hell in the girl's household or not, but it was very obvious. Being around their other family was some of the best moments for Sanity and Keisha. It gave them a lot of quality time to spend together. These were some of the only times they actually got to know each other.

At one point in time, Sanity thought Keisha hated her since they were two grades apart. When they were at school Keisha was also distant with Sanity as if she didn't want to be around her. Keisha had her own set of friends as well as Sanity. There were times they walked past each other at school as if the other one didn't exist. Their friends were very puzzled they would ask questions. Both Keisha and Sanity would say "she didn't speak to me, so I didn't speak to her." These encounters were weird to their friends. As time went on, their friends noticed this was the way they were towards each other and seeing one another every day wasn't a big deal to them.

Although they acted this way towards each other, it was shameful to both of the girls because they would walk with their friends down the hallways of the school, and they would see their siblings. Things were a bit different, and they couldn't wait to get their sibling's attention. They couldn't wait to run to them, they couldn't wait to hug them, they couldn't wait to say, "we're going to go outside at the same time so meet me outside." They couldn't wait for those things.

For Sanity and Keisha things were so much different. They focused on getting to know each other and loving one another. Their friends and siblings would go crazy to get to see them during school, they would jump up and down full of excitement. They would be so excited to say, "oh that's my sister" "oh that's my brother" "oh let's walk down that hall" "my brother's classes are on this hall" "my sister classes on this hall." But for Sanity and her siblings, things were so out of touch, they didn't even press the issue to see their siblings during school hours; it was almost like they were enemies. And that just wasn't the case they actually didn't hate each other. It was just that they learned more about how to be divided, how to not be there for each other, how to stab each other in the back, and how to talk about each other because if anything went on with one of them in those moments.

Catherine spoke to them and had no problem with sitting them down separately to speak bad about the other one. Big Momma and Willie showed them so much love. It made the kids feel different because it wasn't love from their mother. Catherine didn't understand the children's need for their mother's love. It is the most precious thing that a child could be given, and it starts as soon as a child is inside of the womb. All of Catherine and Willie's kids depended on that type of love.

As Sanity and Tim walked slowly from the studio, which was way past their curfew time, they were going back and forth about who was going to ask Willie about the studio. The reason it was so hard to ask him was because Sanity and Tim had been going to the studio recording music for months without anyone knowing and it was working out well. The two were so good at keeping each other's secrets. However, Sanity felt awful for not mentioning the studio let alone the situation with Catherine. She knew how close they were and how they felt about each other but that was the thing that made the situation the most difficult for her. To tell Tim she knew would cause him to turn their house out with rage and anger. He always would have her back. No matter how young Tim was, he was mature for his age and that's why Sanity was able to discuss any and everything with him. Tim could sit down with anyone and carry on a deep conversation like a grown man. His vocabulary was strong for his age. Tim believed in loyalty, love, trust, and honesty. If Sanity ever told Tim what she was feeling and going through, the situation could have gone all the way wrong. If Tim knew what Sanity was going through it would have broken him all the way down.

Chapter 21

Sanity felt it was best to keep the secret between her, Catherine, and God. Catherine and Sanity both knew the guy Catherine was secretly seeing wouldn't ever let their little secret slip out for the simple fact that Willie was so well known around the town. He knew Willie would have done whatever it took to save his family especially his children from any harm being done to them. Sanity lifted her head up, looked at Tim after laughing hard and said, "man forget this. Man, you must be going to ask Willie because I'm scared."

Tim looked back at her, laughed, and said, "shoot me too." They knew once they stepped foot to the door, they knew they would be in big trouble. Normally when the kids would show up late or past curfew Willie had already been out strolling the neighborhood looking to see if they were out playing with their friends. If Willie couldn't keep his eyes on his kids at all times, then he would worry about their safety. Willie had his mean and aggressive ways toward Catherine and sometimes the kids too, but he loved them more than anything in the world.

Alcoholism played a huge part in Willie's behavior at times but through all of it, he never stopped showing his kids how much he loved and would have protected them from anything that was of harm. Being the ideal great father, he would have put all five of his children inside of a bubble to save them from the world. Willie always had the mindset that no one but him can say anything to hurt his kid's feelings. As Sanity and Tim got closer to their house she looked over at Tim and said, "Oh my God we're getting closer. I know we are going to get in trouble, so oh well it is what it is."

Tim looked back at her and said, "I was already thinking that but still we need to figure out how we're going to ask him if we can go to the studio so we can do what Triple O said we should do." Then Tim said, "forget it sis man I'm just going to ask him myself when he calms down because you know he is about to be hot with us right?" Sanity was scared but she was ready for whatever came her way. Tim didn't know that in order to walk in Sanity's shoes, you had to be tough especially with all that she kept on her mind and in her heart. Sanity agreed with him and said, "forget it man we are just going to ask him together and if he says no, we just going to have to figure out a way to keep going but we can't let this chance pass us by."

Triple O already told them if they weren't going to come to the studio to record the next day then he would go out of town to handle some business with some more people. As Sanity and Tim walked up to the porch to knock on the door, Willie was already standing there with the angry look on his face. Before they could say anything he yelled, "where the hell have y'all been? I've been all over the neighborhood looking for y'all. I told y'all not to let the streetlights catch y'all and y'all keep playing with me. Y'all had me worried as hell. Get y'all asses in here I hope you know it'll be a cold day in hell before y'all can go anywhere else. I told y'all to stop playing with me. It is too much going on in these streets for y'all to be coming in anytime y'all want. Y'all ain't grown, got me all worked up and I got to be to work in the morning and y'all asses got to be to school too. What in the hell was y'all thinking? I'm going to show you all I'm not playing with y'all. Now both of you will be on punishment forever. Get in this house, take a bath, and get ready for school. Y'all still going to tell me where the hell y'all been because ain't nobody in the neighborhood seen y'all. You can't say you was out there playing with your friends because I went to all of your friends' houses, and everybody said they haven't seen either one of you at all today. So, tell me where were y'all?" Sanity didn't know what to say. Tim saw the fear in her eyes, so he stepped up and said, "dang okay we were at one of my friend's houses in the country."

Willie asked, "how did you get there?" As bad as Tim wanted to just tell Willie the truth, he didn't. He told him his friend's older brother came and got them from the park. Willie's first words were, "you're a liar." Sanity felt so bad for Tim she blurted out, "it's the truth we really went to his friend's house in the country because we were bored, and his brother came back late to bring us back home. That's why we got in so late."

Willie stood over them with an angry face and said, "so Sanity you're the oldest and you're going to look me dead in my face and tell me a lie?" Sanity immediately started crying because she was full of emotions. She wanted to tell Willie the truth, but she knew he would have been so upset. He wouldn't have understood how much this meant to her at such a young age. Willie wanted all of his kids to get a great education before they thought about doing anything outside of school. Willie was still that overbearing father who wanted to protect them from anything so if he knew that Sanity had been in the studio around a much older guy he would have been upset.

Triple O was trying to make sure Sanity got her voice heard because he believed in her just as much as Tim did. Tim met Triple O while he was hanging with some of his friends at the park one day. Triple O told him he had a studio in his house. Tim told Sanity because she was the first person he thought about. Tim set things up with Triple O letting him know that his sister liked to sing. Before Sanity got to the studio Tim and Triple O had everything ready for her to record. It was almost as if Sanity and Triple O already knew each other forever the feeling was mutual when they met the first time. The last thing Sanity wanted was for Willie to approach Triple O about the wrong thing and mess up her chances of being recorded. She was so comfortable with Triple O he made her feel as if she was the next big thing for the city. She was able to take as long as she needed to warm up before she started recording and every time she messed up, he wouldn't get aggravated or frustrated with her. Anytime she was off tune, he got her back into it and was relaxed while doing so.

Chapter 22

Sanity didn't want to experience the studio with anyone else because she was shy and had a lot of stage fright. She never performed or sang for anyone other than her family and friends. No one in the town knew Sanity had a voice or even had a passion for singing because it was something she hid. Tim wanted to be a rapper, but he always said if he could just have seen Sanity make it, he knew he would have made it. They always considered each other as a duo.

As Willie was yelling at Sanity, she cried harder and harder while trying to catch her breath so she could have told him the truth. At that point, it almost felt impossible for them to be able to get the truth out to see if Willie would really let them continue to go to the studio. The biggest problem was if Willie had found out that they were already going to the studio for months prior to them even asking, they would have gotten in even more trouble.

After Tim and Sanity went ahead and accepted their punishment since they refused to tell Willie the truth, the next day Tim made a way to go back to the studio to talk with Triple O and give him the news that Sanity wouldn't be able to record. He told him they broke their curfew and would be on punishment for a long time. Of course, Triple O felt bad for the both of them, but he asked Tim to deliver a message to Sanity. He wanted Tim to tell Sanity to never give up and whenever she was ready to record no matter how long it took for her to get off of punishment, he would be there to help her. Tim and Sanity felt as if they really had somebody in their corner when it came to their happiness for music. Willie was very stern on what he said about their age and wanting to be in the music industry. He was too overprotective so him saying yes would have been the last thing. He was more upset with Sanity than he was with Tim because Sanity was a girl. Willie felt like his girls needed more protection from the streets than his sons.

Willie was the type of father down for whatever dreams his kids wanted to chase but to him the dreams had to have been age appropriate. Music and acting dreams for Sanity and Tim at the time were not age appropriate according to Willie. This was because Sanity was still a girl and being in the studio would require her to be around a lot of men. Willie did not trust men around his daughters. He did not want anyone rather it be male or female to ever hurt his kids. Sanity was broken into a million pieces without anyone ever knowing. All she did was think about if Willie had found out about the secret that she and Catherine kept between each other and what he would have done. She thought Willie would just walk away and never want anything to do with her again. Willie probably would have harmed Catherine because in his heart and in his mind, he would have felt like Catherine put his little girl Sanity in harm's way. This was something he would never stand for from anyone.

There were times Willie stopped Sanity and her siblings from going over to family members' houses if he felt that they were being mistreated or looked over. Willie didn't know his aggressiveness made things a little hard for the kids. If they needed a break and wanted to spend the weekend with their cousins Willie would fuss. Their Aunts and Uncles were already fed up with Willie approaching every situation aggressively. These situations did not help Sanity's anxiety or depression that he knew nothing about. Whenever she would go with her family on the weekends it felt like a breath of fresh air for her and Keisha, as said before.

Two years later, Sanity finally got used to high school the best she knew how. High school for Sanity was different from middle school because she was forced to be around more people, more classes, and different personalities. This was hard for Sanity to cope with. Being around a lot of people made Sanity very nervous. She always was that way. She knew if she had made it really big, she would have had to do big performances. She always kept in mind that she did not want to crack in front of a crowd of people, so she also dealt with that.

Chapter 23

Sanity always knew, if she explained exactly how she felt inside to someone, about what she was going through, and where her mindset was at her age. No one would have ever understood. She felt she would have just been talking to herself. Sanity wasn't the only one who dreamed big. Her friends also had dreams; they just never spoke about it as much. Most individuals around Sanity's age had some of the same dreams and aspirations that Sanity had. Most of the kids she grew up with had the mentality of an adult. Most of the adults in the family worked a lot so they didn't have the time to sit down with their kids and find out exactly what each child wanted to do with their life.

Because high school was so different from middle school and so many classes were given, Sanity got a chance to see Joe and Keisha every day. They all were only one to two grades apart, but things didn't change with how they acted towards one another. Even years later they still walked past each other as if they didn't exist to each other. Whenever they would walk past each other in the hallways, they all had the same look on their face. The look was a look of disappointment and embarrassment. Sanity began to think Joe and Keisha were holding onto the same feelings inside thinking to themselves, *why are we like this with each other, why can't we be like our friends and their siblings?* Sanity felt her and Keisha's bond was growing closer but for Joe it was always a dead end. He acted as if he wanted nothing to do with any of his siblings. This left Sanity,

Keisha, and Tim to wonder if he actually hated them for real.

As the days passed, things got worse for Sanity. She craved more attention from Catherine while seeking more attention from any and everybody who would give it to her. It did not matter if it was bad attention or good attention. Although she hated being around large crowds of people, she felt the need to pull the attention in from them. This is when her life started to take a turn in the wrong direction. After a few days of taking packages of homework home and asking Catherine for help, Catherine shut her out once again by yelling at her. Catherine would always say she should have paid attention in school, and she was not helping her with shit. Sanity thought it was weird enough Catherine never asked any of them if they had any homework or how school was. The only person who would ask them was their father Willie and Big Momma. Big Momma wasn't too fond of schoolwork. She was older and Willie spent so much time working long hours so that he could help provide for the family that by the time he got off from work, it was time for them to go to bed.

Whenever the kids would go back to school with their work not completed, the school staff started to become more involved in figuring out what was really going on with them. Staff started sending notes home and calls to home letting Catherine know they needed to have a parent teacher conference. No matter how much in school suspension Sanity got for trying to fit in with the wrong crowd, she would continue to do the same things over and over. Sanity would not be compliant when staff members would ask her about specific incidents that caused her to get in trouble.

Sanity captured the heart of one of the guidance counselors at the high school that she attended and for some reason the guidance counselor loved Sanity as if she was her own. The counselor tried hard to get through to Sanity; she would even pull her out of class during testing to let her test in her office. She wanted to see if she could get a feel of why Sanity was behaving the way she was. The guidance counselor then began to reflect there was something going on inside of Sanity's home and she wanted to dig deeper. The only way to dig deeper was to get Catherine in for a parent teacher conference to explain that Sanity was in jeopardy of being flunked. She wanted to know if there was anything going on inside the home that was preventing Sanity from giving her best in school.

Catherine would agree to the conference day and time but would never show up. When Sanity would go to school the next day the counselor would come and pull her out of class to ask if Catherine was going to show up for the conference. Sanity did not want to lie to the counselor because it's safe to say that she had developed more trust in the counselor at that time then she did Catherine. Sanity told the counselor Catherine would not come to the conference. The counselor asked, "Sanity, why do you call your mother by her name?" This was a red flag for the counselor because it wasn't normal for kids to call their parents by their names. Sanity

wanted nothing more than to tell the guidance
counselor what was really going on with her but in
the midst of it all she had already begun to be numb
to any and everything that was going on around her.
Every time the counselor would question her about
her behavior, she had no explanation for why. She
couldn't seem to get it together no matter what
the consequences were.

Chapter 24

Sanity had already developed a strong mindset no matter what her situation looked like. She would not stop doing whatever it took to get out. She considered getting out of her whole situation, not just the town that she grew up in, but the toxic mindset she was in as well. Every day was an uphill battle for Sanity and truth be told it was for her siblings as well. Sanity tried so hard to fight for Catherine's love but there wasn't one time that she wasn't rejected by her. It created scars on her heart simply because Sanity couldn't understand why Catherine treated her and her siblings this way.

Sanity spent most of her days trying to figure Catherine out while at the same time admiring her beauty. She wanted to look up to Catherine, but it was so obvious that Catherine didn't want anything to do with Sanity. This broke Sanity's spirit and she felt as if Catherine hated her. At that moment she felt as if there was no need to try to love Catherine because she wouldn't love her back. She started to feel like the world was laughing at her because of all of the things that she was going through. There seemed to be no way out. After a while, Sanity started to feel hopeless as she was starting to not understand her own behavior. She was doing crazy things and skipping class became the norm for her. She even went as far as skipping school all together.

Sanity hung out with a group of girls she loved dearly and a few of them had in-house issues. One of her friend's mom showed her a lot of love but then she would beat on her every chance she got.

There were moments when her friend would come to school with a black eye. Sanity never would have thought anyone in her circle of friends would have had as many problems as she had at home. In Sanity's mind, she thought that getting beat on by Catherine would have been much better than what Catherine was putting her through. After spending an entire day with the school guidance counselor, Mrs. Jacobs, Sanity started to warm up to her. Mrs. Jacobs asked, "what do you want to do with your life? Because you're not complying with school rules and your behavior is unacceptable."

Sanity looked in her eyes and said, "at this point I don't know what I want to do with my life. I mean I wanted to do music, but I don't think that will happen."

"Why?" Mrs. Jacobs asked. After the second question Sanity shut down holding so much in and didn't know how to let it out the right way. All she knew was at that time she had some attention from another woman that seemed to love and care for her more than Catherine did. It seemed like it would have been easier to open up to Mrs. Jacobs but instead it was much harder for her. Sanity still did not want the world to look at Catherine any different than they already saw her. Regardless of what Catherine did to her, Sanity wanted nothing more than to love her and be loved in return.

Catherine thought what she was giving her kids was enough. She would say, "y'all owe me y'all life because I had y'all." Sanity felt like maybe she was right, she did owe her everything. Even with the unforeseen things that took place that only Catherine, God and Catherine's love Jimmie knew about. Any of the things Catherine would say when no one was paying attention or not around definitely stuck with Sanity for many years.

Getting off of the school bus one afternoon Sanity heard Tim yell from the top of the hill as Sanity, Keisha, and Joe were getting off. Sanity opened her eyes wide while holding one finger to her dark full-size lips. She was holding her finger as still as she could because she was afraid of Tim saying something about the studio in front of Keisha and Joe. Sanity had every bad thought running through her head but all she could do was say a silent prayer as she walked closer to Tim. Once they got close enough, she ran to him with a nervous puzzled look on her face not knowing what Tim would say next. All she knew was she needed to get to him before he mentioned Triple O or anything about the studio. Sanity then whispered to Tim, "oh my God please don't say anything about us going to the studio."

Tim looked at her and said, "now sis you know I know not to say nothing stop playing girl!" He chuckled thinking it was funny. Sanity would even think he would let it be known that they spend long days in the studio without their parents knowing.

Chapter 25

Over the years Sanity had gotten bad with trust issues and that meant that no one was trusted in Sanity's eyes. She knew she could trust Tim but there still was a little voice in the back of her head that told her no one should be trusted. She felt bad for second guessing Tim. She knew better than to think he would have said something to or in front of Keisha or Joe. Sanity didn't want them to know because Joe always walked around like the world owed him something and no one knew why. Joe would flip out on whoever would ask any questions about him or his life. Sanity made sure she stayed away from any topics that had anything to do with Joe. She was already dealing with hiding her own demons.

As Sanity and Tim walked up a few steps ahead of Keisha and Joe they whispered still trying to figure out how they would get around Catherine and Willie knowing they were hanging out in a studio with older guys. They didn't really worry about Catherine; it was Willie that kept them on their toes daily. There were a lot of things the kids could have gotten away with if it was up to Catherine because she didn't pay much attention to them anyway.

When Sanity got her first menstrual cycle at the age of thirteen, she had forgotten everything that Big Momma had told her about caring for herself when that time came because her mind stayed clouded. As Sanity was getting out of the bed early that morning to get ready for school in her long white tee shirt and white panties, Keisha noticed that Sanity had a lot of blood on the back of her panties. She yelled, "omg Sanity you have blood everywhere!" Sanity was happy to finally get her menstrual for some odd reason. It made her feel like she finally was able to fit in with her other friends at school. Sanity heard Catherine getting something to drink out of the refrigerator and said to her, "Catherine my period started." Catherine looked at her in disgust and yelled for Willie. Sanity felt embarrassed and confused because she did not feel comfortable with men knowing about her cycle, even her own father.

Willie came to the kitchen where Sanity and Catherine stood and said, "yea you called me Catherine?"

Catherine looked at Willie with a mean look on her face as if Sanity had just made the worst mistake of her life like having her cycle was in her control. "Oh, yea this girl done started her period." The whole time she was telling Willie this, her back was facing Sanity. Sanity was used to watching Catherine's back in more ways than one. Willie looked at Catherine for about a minute then he yelled and said, "Sanity go clean yourself up." Sanity cried because she knew that Willie wasn't upset with her for something she could not control. He was pissed with Catherine for calling him to do what a mother should have done in that moment. Willie was used to it, but it frustrated him at the same time. He saw the embarrassment on Sanity's face while she was crying out of shame.

Sanity felt Catherine knew exactly what she was doing to embarrass her, but Sanity never said a word about it. Once she got to school, she finally opened up to one of her close friends and told her what happened and how she felt about it. Most of the time it was better not to say anything because no one seemed to care or had believed her. Sanity had every reason to keep a lot of things to herself. It was safer with her because she was still a child in the world's eyes. Catherine had painted Sanity to be a liar to the world while she worked on using her as a scapegoat for her own personal pleasures. There were plenty of times Big Momma would also say, "Sanity, stop lying. Catherine said all you do is lie." Sanity put it all together over the years and realized it wasn't until the prison visits and sitting in a room all day overthinking things was when Sanity figured out she was targeted by her own mother.

Catherine would bribe Sanity with getting her hair done and Sanity was still holding on to this part. It gave her an opportunity to hang out with her friends a little more. Getting by with things right under Catherine's nose was the norm for Sanity and her siblings. After all of the kids got closer to their home, Tim decided he wasn't going in the house. He said that he would be back later after he met up with his friends. Sanity knew Tim probably went to see Triple O about getting her into the studio. Sanity always felt her heart beating really fast over the years but the only time she could remember Catherine taking her to the doctor was to get her on birth control. After a visit or two to the doctor Sanity had to depend on her cousin Tiesha to take her and help her keep up with her appointments. They were both the same age, attended the same school, and hung out a lot when Sanity's aunt would come over and visit. Tiesha was her aunt's only daughter at the time, so she was always with her. Sanity and Tiesha were so close because Sanity felt she was the only other person she could have trusted with her secrets. Sanity still tried to protect Catherine's character and feelings.

Chapter 26

Tiesha never knew what Sanity was going through because when she and her mom would come over to visit, Catherine put on the biggest fake smile and made it look like she loved her kids to the outside world. Thank God for Big Momma because the whole time Catherine thought she was getting away with her lies, the entire family knew different. There were times when Tiesha and Sanity would sit on the front porch and Tiesha would say, "when are you getting your hair done again" or "I know Catherine taking y'all school shopping right?" Since the two were close, Sanity knew what Tiesha was getting at. Sanity never came out and said what she really wanted to say.

Willie was definitely fed up with not seeing where all of the money he faithfully gave Catherine every week for the kids. She never really had anything to show for because she made sure she went the cheap route. She would take the girls to the hair school and spend eight to ten dollars max. Catherine was always cheap when it came to providing for them. Catherine got away with telling Willie she paid way more than what she actually did to get the girl's hair done. There was times Catherine didn't even take the girls to the school for a hair appointment because she had a friend from the projects that would do the girl's hair every so often. Willie, of course, believed every word she said just because the girl's hair looked different from when he last saw them.

It didn't take much to put a big smile on Willie's face. All he needed was to see his girls look beautiful. He would fuss all day and night if the girls weren't taken care of. He knew it wasn't a question when it came to Big Momma, but Catherine kept him yelling about something, especially when it came to all of their kids. It would have been him fussing about their homework or Sanity's hair being all over her head. Catherine became another bully to Sanity because if Sanity would walk through the house with her hair looking horrible Catherine would be the first person to say, "damn girl your head look a mess." This would cause the other kids to call Sanity names like Beetle Juice.

Sanity couldn't stand being called names because she would have to go through this at school. Sanity walked around withholding so much pain. Some days it was normal for her but on others she felt like she was having a fist fight with the devil himself that was never-ending. As the streetlights were coming on, Tim came running down the street yelling his favorite words. When he got close to the house he yelled, "Sanity sis lets walk to the store. I raked some people's yards today so we can go get some snacks." Sanity was so excited because she knew Tim wanted her to walk to the store for more than one reason. Judging by the look on Tim's face, something had made his day. Sanity went into the house to ask Big Momma if she needed anything from the store. She said, "now gal you know I need a few things from the store."

Sanity took pride in going to the store for Big Momma because she knew she would be able to get anything she wanted from her if Big Momma would allow her to keep the change and not mention it to the other kids. Big Momma handed Sanity the money and made her repeat what was on the list a couple of times before she walked back outside. Tim waited on her outside. One thing about Big Momma, she could read facial expressions and body language like no other. She looked at Sanity up and down and said, "tuh where are you trying to rush to?"

Sanity laughed and said, "Ma! Give me the money I ain't rushing. I just don't want the streetlights to catch us, you know we are not trying to get in trouble."

Big Momma said, "trouble by who? Hell, ain't nothing going to happen if I send y'all girl you must be crazy."

Chapter 27

If Big Momma sends the kids to the store and they came in after dark, Willie was okay with the late store runs for Big Momma but not Catherine. After a few years passed, Willie was on board with Catherine's tricks; he didn't even trust the kids going to the store for Catherine anymore because she became very suspicious to him and by this time Sanity had turned sixteen years old. She had a little bit more freedom but the catch to it was only if Big Momma vouched for her. Sanity would go to Big Momma and have her ask Willie could she go certain places. Tim walked in the house and gave Sanity a look as if he was getting frustrated while talking through his teeth, "oh my God Sanity! We have to go before the store close." He wanted to talk to Sanity alone and she knew exactly what he wanted to talk about.

Big Momma stared at Tim out the corner of her eyes and said, "tuh! Y'all think y'all slick? I know when something ain't right and Tim you're looking real anxious so what y'all up too? And ya bet not lie!" Sanity already knew that look on Big Momma's face meant that Big Momma already knew something was not right with them. Sanity felt the need to tell her their little secret about going back-and-forth to the studio. Sanity was very nervous before she opened her mouth to tell Big Momma her and Tim's secret but that didn't stop her. At the end of the day, she knew if she could trust anyone else it would be Big Momma making it a lot easier tell her.

Sanity blurted out, "Big Momma we've been going to the studio for a while now but you have got to promise us that you will not tell Willie or Catherine anything about it!"

Big Momma then looked up at Sanity with a small smirk on her face and said, "girl get on out of here you know I ain't going to say nothing about it, but you better be careful because people do try to take advantage of young kids especially little girls and what kind a studio is this anyway?"

"It's the kind of studio that you go and record music in Big Momma. You know I love music and you know I had to find a way. But Big Momma you gotta promise us that you won't tell because you know Willie will be so upset with us and stop us from going. Besides, me and Tim are working on a master plan for our whole family." It came to a point where Sanity knew that deep down inside Tim wanted to do it for the whole entire family. Sanity pushed further and further away from her family. She still felt she needed to do what she needed to do for her and Tim only. Sanity always felt like if she had made it big that there were only a select few people she would carry with her along the way while Tim thought that his way was the right way.

Every day the thought of carrying the entire family stayed on Sanity's mind. As much as she wanted to look at it the way that Tim was looking at it, she just couldn't get past the hurt and pain she had endured from Catherine early on. Tim knew something deep, and dark was bothering Sanity and she just wasn't speaking about it. As they would walk to the store Tim said, "dang Sanity how the heck you let Big Momma talk you into telling her what we got going on? You are so soft sis. I'm not trying to be funny sis but ain't no way you let her scare you into telling. Oh my God, I swear you was the one that stayed on my back about it and just look at ya! But it's okay I don't think she will say anything about it." The whole time Tim is laughing and in Sanity's mind she was thinking, *damn I shouldn't have said anything, but it was too late the secret had already been told.* The good thing was it was told to someone she trusted more than life itself. Sanity didn't tell Tim she was worried about it after they walked away. She just played it cool and gave him a look that for sure let him know that she was going to be chill until he got through laughing and having his little moment of crying laughing at her for breaking for Big Momma.

Tim grabbed Sanity by the arm and said, "okay I'm going to stop laughing at you but that was too funny watching you stumble all over your words while Big Momma was drilling us for answers. You looked like you were scared. I told you before Sanity, your face tells it all every time," Tim said while shaking his head back and forth slowly. Tim was in disbelief that Sanity broke that easy especially about sneaking out and how hard she was on him. He just couldn't believe that it was so easy for her to let the cat out of the bag, as Big Momma would have said and that meant telling a secret.

Chapter 28

Sanity felt crazy for telling Big Momma. She looked over at Tim and yelled, "boy ain't nothing that funny you can stop laughing now! I didn't know what to tell her. I felt like she already knew that's why she was asking so hell I told her." She burst out laughing with him because they both knew she was telling the truth.

"No but for real Sanity I spoke to Triple O and he really, really, really believes that we can do this so that's what we're going to do. We can't stop now we have come too far. With Triple O behind us, I think we can pull this thing off but the truth is we are going to have to keep sneaking to the studio. Ain't no way Catherine or Willie gonna be okay with that. As long as we don't get caught, we will be fine I promise you." Sanity agreed with Tim without a doubt.

She said, "I'm scared but it's all worth it. I will take that ass whooping if that's what it takes to follow my dreams because I've been waiting for a long time for this opportunity. If we don't do this now, who knows, this chance may never come again. To be honest I'm tired of just dreaming to be someone different just to please everyone else but myself. Now is the time we do exactly what we want to do and trust me bro, in the end they will be happy for us."

"Heck yeah so this is what we are going to do, we are going to go hard this week and get the album done but you got to stay on point Sanity!" Tim had a serious look on his face drawing Sanity closer to the beautiful idea of becoming everything she always wanted to be. Sanity knew if Tim said it was a great idea, then she was all for it at any cost. Before they knew it, the streetlights had come on. Their anxiety was high because they knew they would have to come up with a story as to what took them so long just to walk to a store only three blocks away. They never even made it to the store because they were talking so much.

As they were walking home, reality kicked in and Tim started laughing. "Sis I'm not worried and you shouldn't be either because you know we always wiggle our way out of getting into too much trouble."

"Tim how we be wiggling our way out of trouble and we stay in trouble when we don't make our curfew. We get caught looking crazy because we can't come up with a reason why we ain't made it home on time? And it looks like in the next few minutes we are going to be in the same situation because we do not have a good reason. So, since you think that we can get out of this one I am going to let you talk the whole time. When Willie starts yelling and asking where we've been you better have a good dang on answer because I'm not saying anything."

They got closer to the house and their hearts were beating out of their chests. Sanity tried every minute of the day to think positive and do what was right, but her surroundings made her feel like it was wrong. She was too scared of telling anyone because they would have only thought she was crazy or insane for having big dreams. She felt most her dreams were a joke mainly because there were very few even interested in knowing what her dreams were overall. The craziest part of it all was Tim was the only one who knew something was bothering her because Sanity was acting out" or either "acting distant for some reason."

When they arrived at their house, they looked over at one another and laughed because they knew that they were running out of lies. They hoped Big Momma didn't get worried about them taking so long to come back and told Willie what they were doing.

"Yooo," Tim yelled out so that anyone in the house would know that it was them at the door.

"Hold on Sand, I'm coming." Keisha yelled back from the other side of the door. As soon as she opened the door, she had this aggressive look on her face that they were too familiar with.

She said, "I hope y'all know y'all are in trouble because Willie left here very mad with both of you. Y'all know better. Y'all act like y'all got a serious problem. Y'all asses stay in trouble." She shook her head and walked away. The older Keisha got the more mature she became, and it showed because she started trying to keep all of her siblings in line and on the right track. Sanity did not like that because she got even angrier with Catherine. It just seemed like everyone else was on board but Catherine.

When Tim and Sanity got all the way in the house, they walked past Catherine's room and saw that she was in the mirror doing her hair. As they walked into Big Momma's room, she looked up at them from her bed. She was combing her beautiful, black, fine curly hair. She also shook her head and said, "Lord I don't know what I'm going to do with the two of you. And I ain't covering for y'all no more because y'all will have me arguing with folks about y'all mess so no I will not do this again. Y'all daddy came in here looking for y'all and I had to tell him a lie and y'all know I'm not a liar. Now one thing I can stand is lying on or to anybody so y'all got me real pissed right now." This made both Tim and Sanity feel bad.

Everyone knew Big Momma hated to even suspect anyone of lying. She would always say, "I can't stand a liar!" She would talk about it all day if you lied to her or if she was forced to lie to protect someone else. They tried apologizing to Big Momma, but she was still upset with them, so she just stayed quiet while staring at them. Tim always thought when Big Momma was mad it was the funniest thing.

A few days passed, and Triple O was prepared to help Sanity and Tim get to where he felt they should have been with their talent. Tim forgot all about why he was into music so much because he was so into seeing Sanity shine bright. He supported her the whole way through and did anything in his power to get his sister's career off of the ground. He even went around to neighborhoods to do lawn care for the elderly in the community just to have enough money to put towards studio time but luckily Triple O wanted nothing more than for them to have made it big. He made sure no matter how long they needed in the studio, it would have been free of charge.

After a long stressful day at school the next day Sanity went home with a lot on her mind. She wondered what life would have become in the next few years. Sanity was known for sleeping a lot, but they never knew why she slept so much. She would always hear that she must be knocked up by some boy from school and that wasn't the case because little did they know, Sanity was not into boys. All she thought about was a way out of the struggle and an escape from her pain. Before she knew it, Sanity slept the whole day away. Her pager received a message from Triple O asking if her and Tim would be at the studio that night. The message had her puzzled because her and Tim had not discussed going to record especially after being in hot water for the last incident.

Tim stayed over at a friend's house the night before and wasn't there. Sanity walked down the hall to attempt to use the landline phone to try and call Triple O. Sanity went to Keisha's room to sleep while she wasn't there after wrecking her brain trying to find a way to get in touch with Tim or Triple O. As Sanity drifted off to sleep, she heard a tapping noise on the window. She quickly jumped out of the bed and tiptoed to the window. To her surprise it was Tim standing there with a big smile on his face smelling like cigarettes.

"Tim, boy you stink. You smell like smoke." Sanity whispered and started laughing, "boy what in the world are you doing out here this time of night. I thought you was staying with your friend tonight."

Tim replied, "yeah that's what I told Willie and that's what he think. I had to say that so that I could come back and get you after I spoke to Triple O. He says he is ready right now."

"Wait what do you mean Tim I'm not dressed. It's late and we got school tomorrow. You are crazy."

"Oh yeah I forgot you won't be at school, right?" Tim's eyes were low. He laughed at everything as he ate chips from his hand.

Sanity shook her head and said, "oh my God Tim you are high ain't you?"

Tim spit all of his chips out laughing at Sanity's question. "Okay sis yes I am. I smoked some weed. You happy now? Come on let's go O is waiting on us and you know we can't get caught."

The one thing Sanity was scared of was the closest friend Catherine had lived right next door to them and he was her one and only best friend which was ok with Willie because he wasn't into women. He would take Catherine to see her lover before and after he went to prison although he knew Willie really well. Catherine would paint a horrible picture of Willie to her friend which caused him to hate Willie. He made sure it was known and Catherine would be so amused.

As Tim helped Sanity climb out of the window, she thought she saw the neighbor peeping through his curtain, but she said to herself it was too late for him to be up. This became regular for them, and it went on for months without anyone knowing. After all of the sneaking out going to the studio things were finally coming together. Keisha got pregnant and moved out. She moved into an apartment complex through public housing because she wasn't working at the time. Sanity was proud of her sister for moving. She told Keisha she would be over her house all the time, but Sanity was so busy with the studio and school. It was hard to keep up with everything, but Tim and Triple O kept pushing her and she kept going.

Before she knew it, she replaced her meals with music and read up on acting in stage plays. Her weight changed, her body began to look like a woman, her attitude changed, and school got worse for her. At sixteen Sanity began to figure out what life really was like. She got older and didn't care about people if they would speak to her any kind of way. After a few years of trips to the prison with Catherine and her best friend, Sanity told Catherine she couldn't go once her heart was starting to feel very numb towards Catherine and her best friend.

Catherine couldn't stand the fact that Sanity might have said something about what she had put her through for years. It bothered Sanity because she thought after all of what Catherine had done to her, she would have treated her like a little princess. All Sanity wanted to do was have a loving bond with Catherine, but she was so stuck in her own feelings and the kids' feelings didn't matter at all. Sanity and Tim spent more time at the studio than school. The studio became their second home away from home. After a long night at the studio, Sanity was in her bed asleep and heard a light knock at the room door. She looked over and noticed it was Catherine. She yelled, "it's me Catherine." Sanity rolled her eyes because in her mind she knew Catherine was going to force her to be her lookout again. She was prepared to flip like never before because the older she got the more fed up she was with everything going on in her life. But surprisingly that's not what Catherine wanted but to Sanity she felt like it wasn't any better. Catherine had another agenda for her.

Chapter 29

"What you doing Catherine," asked Sanity as she stood in her doorway acting sleepier than she really was. She hoped Catherine wouldn't ask her why she hadn't been to school all week but that wasn't what Catherine wanted. She wanted to tell Sanity she knew about her and Tim sneaking out of the window going to the studio because of the neighbor. The night Sanity thought the neighbor was watching he told Catherine the very next day. Catherine's exact words to Sanity was, "I know your slick sneaky ass is jumping out of your window at night with some boy! And don't you stand here and look to me." Sanity folded her arms and looked Catherine in her face for a few seconds before she even responded. She was ready for whatever Catherine brought her way.

"What are you talking about Catherine? What boy am I sneaking out the house with please tell me that?" Sanity's blood was on fire as she stood there. She knew if Catherine knew she was sneaking away from the house with someone at night, then she knew exactly who it was. And Catherine already knew that as well, but she knew that she had to come at Sanity from another angle by blackmailing her.

Sanity wanted nothing more than to stay out of trouble and walk a straight path. She didn't want to get in any trouble by Willie and she knew that she really wanted to tell Catherine how she really felt.

"So let me guess, you are going to tell my daddy that I was sneaking out of the house at night with some random boy, right?" Catherine's response was straight forward. She looked at Sanity and said, "do I need to tell Willie what's been going on with you and this sneaking out?" Sanity became very angry inside and wanted to expose Catherine right then and there, but she was torn between will anyone believe her or will Willie forgive her for not saying something sooner. She dismissed the thought of telling because she felt any word that came out of her mouth was a lie in the family eyes. Catherine had a very conniving spirit, and she knew how to get anyone she came in contact with to believe every lie she told or cover up. Sanity felt that Catherine was surely the mastermind behind her pain.

"Sanity don't stand there looking at me with those big ass eyes you know exactly what I'm talking about. You think you slick sneaking out the window with some boy all times of night. Hell yeah. I'm going to tell Willie because you know better. I just don't know what got into you." Sanity's eyes watered but she didn't cry because she was too angry to cry.

She walked away from the door yelling, "alright Catherine if that's what you want to believe, then believe it." She pushed the door shut. Sanity didn't feel bad for walking away because Catherine already knew the truth. Sanity was more motivated after being so close to getting caught for her late-night studio sessions. Three days later, Sanity was back in the same routine where Tim would leave the house giving the impression that he was going over to his best friend's house but would wait until Sanity let him know everyone in the house was asleep to help her escape. That night Tim had a different way of helping Sanity sneak out. He brought his best friend along and the plan went smooth. Tim's best friend Chase knocked at the neighbor's back door to distract him from seeing Tim help Sanity jump out of her window. They already knew he was the one who told Catherine what was going on. By the time Chase walked back to the front of the house, Sanity and Tim were long gone up the street to the park. Once Chase got closer, Tim yelled softly to let Chase know that they were standing behind the sliding board in the park.

"Oh my God," Sanity blurted out. "Tim, do you think anyone seen us?"

"No girl stop being so scary we about to go around this corner and get the music recorded and get back to the house before it's time for us to get up for school or before anyone notices that you're gone." As soon as they got to the studio Triple O was pumped and ready to record but Sanity was still worked up from Catherine already saying something to her about sneaking out. Tim had to keep reminding her it was a dream and she needed to loosen up and get to the music. Sanity always felt better when Tim would encourage her to go hard for her dreams. Sanity grabbed the mic and tapped it three times to make sure it was on. "Okay y'all ready?" Sanity spoke into the mic with a tremble in her voice.

Triple O responded, "yeah Sanity but are you ready?"

"Yeah, let's do this. I'm born ready," she replied with a smirk on her face.

As soon as they were done recording the song Tim asked, "so what's the name of this song?"

Sanity said, "the name of that song will be *Because of the Pain*." The song was about the kind of pain from one lover to the other. The song described the damaging relationships between a man and his lover. It was the kind of pain that turned a woman's heart cold because of some type of abuse in their relationship. Why Sanity had chosen to write a song like that, she didn't even know. All she knew was that anything that caused any type of pain to anyone she wanted to turn it into music no matter who was experiencing pain. She wanted others to be able to relate to her lyrics.

Triple O stood up face to face with Sanity and smiled, "girl you going to be something else out here. You're too grown for your own age. Oh yeah, I saw your mom yesterday with her pretty self. I told her you were a beast in the studio she was so happy she started asking me a thousand questions about how long y'all be in here recording so I told her sometimes all night. She said she was going to start coming with y'all to see how well you do on the microphone."

"What the hell," Sanity yelled. "What do you mean you told her we be here all night? Oh my God she was not supposed to know that we be here! They are not okay with me pursuing music at my age and they damn sure don't know that we are coming here late nights. My daddy will kill us if this gets back to him. Lord what are we going to do now Tim?" Tim sat there puzzled. The whole time Sanity was panicking and yelling because this was one situation he knew he couldn't get them out of.

Tim stood up. "Okay sis calm down. Man, you making it worse so chill and let's come up with something quick and get you back in the house before she goes looking for you." Sanity's anxiety was all over the place. Tim said, "forget it man. I'm just going to tell them all of this was my idea and I boosted you up to do it."

"No Tim. I can't let you take all of the blame and to be honest you're only supporting my dreams so it's all my fault because I'm the only recording not you."

"Yeah sis but I'm a man I can take it you can't. Let's just put it all on me."

"First of all, stop right there. You are not a man, little boy you are younger than me, so I put the blame on me. Hell, why not. I get blamed for everything anyway," as she shrugged her shoulders.

"Man whatever," Tim said as he and Triple O were laughing. Wait what so you telling me that y'all parents did not know the whole time y'all were coming here to record? Aww man that's what you call ambition and determination like for real. That alone tells me that y'all two young asses are hungry for this and that means that y'all are going to do big things if you connect with the right people." Sanity felt maybe he was right and the only way to get in contact with the right people would need an adult signature for everything.

She looked at Tim and said, "it is what it is. I will take whatever punishment I get."

Tim said, "yeah but if we go on punishment again how will we finish recording?"

"We will make a way. I like acting too. Maybe we can record on a tape recorder and send it to Tyler Perry or It's *Show Time at the Apollo* or something. I just know one thing we can't stop now. We came too far so if it means getting in trouble then oh well. Now like I said I'll take the punishment but we're gonna have to try to find another way to make it."

"Okay Sanity then that's a deal. That's what we are going to have to do. Well let's go ahead on and make it back home before they find out you left again tonight."

"Alright my bad, I'm sorry y'all Triple O said I didn't know y'all people didn't know y'all was coming over but even so, I still got y'all back. If they ask me, I will tell them y'all ain't been back over here since the last time I saw your mother."

Tim said, "alright bro you're okay you didn't know and we appreciate everything you do for us. We will holla at you later." As Tim and Sanity walked away from Triple O's place you could tell the both of them were so scared because they knew there was no way out of this one.

Tim said, "man sis forget it. Let's just tell them the truth, what can they do? It's just music dang."

Sanity said, "again Tim you don't understand I am too young to make my own decisions so that means I would need them to sign everything for me giving their permission. So, think about what you're saying, do you think that Willie would really let me go out of town if I have to be with people I don't know and way older than me?"

"Dang I didn't even think about that because I thought that if you say you want to do it you can."

"No boy that's not how that goes because if that was the case, I would have told them and said forget it and leave the house whenever I wanted to go to the studio."

"Well okay maybe if we go to them together and you break everything down to them then they will understand how much we love this."

"Oh my God Tim what don't you understand? It's just not that easy and you know that. I don't know why you keep saying telling them would be the right thing to do. Forget it we just need to wait and see what happens."

"You're right sis," Tim replied while they walked around to the side of the house. Sanity's window was pushed down a little giving them the impression that something wasn't right. One thing that Sanity always made sure she did was left her window up so that it would be easier for her to get back through.

Tim was the first to say, "Wait sis something ain't right. Now I know for sure we left that window up higher than we always do so somebody had been in your room."

"Oh God. I bet it was Catherine," Sanity said.

"Sanity man I'm tired of hiding and sneaking if they ask us, we just going to tell them so go ahead on in there and act normal." Once Sanity climbed back through the window, she shut it, put her night clothes and laid down in the bed. Before she could fall asleep there was a knock at her door. Her heart started racing because she knew that was the moment of truth that Catherine had known all about it all along and was going to try to make sure that Willie knew.

Chapter 30

"Who is it?" Sanity yelled playing like she was asleep.

"Girl don't play with me it's me Catherine!"

"It's unlocked, come in," said Sanity.

As soon as Catherine entered the room and closed the door she said, "girl all you do is lie now I asked you were you sneaking out the window with a boy and you lied right to my face. So, who is the boy that you been sneaking out with all times of the night and don't make me ask you again?"

Sanity stared at Catherine for a few seconds and then said, "Catherine do you really think or believe I was sneaking out of the window at night with some random boy or are you just trying to get me in trouble by Willie? Because you and I both know that's not even me to be sneaking out of a window just to see a random boy."

"Well, who is the boy then and where the hell do you be going with him?"

"So, you really going to keep saying I'm sneaking out with a boy?" Sanity was getting more annoyed with just listening to Catherine's false accusations she was trying so hard to come up with. All she could hear in her head was Tim's voice saying, just tell them the truth if they ever asked. So that's what pumped Sanity up to tell Catherine the truth and given the fact Catherine already knew because of her run in with Triple O a few days earlier.

"Catherine, I already know you know what's been going on, so I'm not going to lie. Me and Tim been going to the studio around the corner for a while now and I'm sure you knew that. If I was sneaking out it was not with some random boy. Even after Triple O told you about me and Tim coming to the studio you still came in here asking me about some boy knowing it was Tim. That's why we don't tell y'all nothing now, because y'all always make a big deal out of it thinking something bad is going to happen to us. I know you are going to tell my daddy so okay."

"No Sanity. I'm not going to tell Willie nothing but the next time you plan on going I want to go so I can see what this studio stuff is about. I won't tell anybody, okay Sanity?"

"Okay Catherine," Sanity replied. Catherine turned to walk away from the room. This left Sanity feeling that there was no way things went that smoothly with telling Catherine and there not be consequences behind her and Tim's actions. Sanity warned Tim she told Catherine the truth so that he could have already been on board with everything.

A week later the family came over to see Big Momma. Of course, in the mix of the crowd was Sanity's favorite cousin Tiesha. She knew that day would be a great day. The family mingled through the house and the teens were all on the porch talking. "Yooo!" Tim could be heard yelling from the top of the street they lived on. Sanity finally felt free after telling Catherine about her and Tim's late-night runs. As soon as Tim got up the stairs and put one foot in the porch, he said "sis come here I got some good news to tell you, and you are going to love this!"

Sanity jumped up as fast as she could because she knew that if Tim said the news was good then it was good for sure. They walked around to the back of the house where no one was so they could talk in private. Tim said, "okay sis I ran into O earlier today he said that he needs you to come and finish the song and he has a place uptown where you need to go to do a photo shoot for the cover of your album."

"Tim stop playing," Sanity yelled jumping up and down just knowing that this was the moment she was waiting for. "Tim, you bet not be playing or lying boy because you know this is not funny."

"Girl I swear I'm not lying I wouldn't even play with you like that."

"Okay so how about I just tell Catherine since she already know because she promised me that she wouldn't tell on me if I just let her know from now on."

"Yeah, you should just make sure she's not around no one else and did Big Momma ever ask you about it again?"

"No," Sanity replied

"Okay, I'm about to go in there and pull her in another room and first ask her if I could go and will she sign papers for me if I need her to. Wish me luck," Sanity said, nudging Tim in the arm.

"You got it sis go ahead and see what she says. I'm about to go and clown with the fam on the front porch so let me know what she says."

"Okay I'm going now," Sanity said, and they went their separate ways. Catherine was standing right by the back door with her back turned towards the door making it much easier for Sanity to pull Catherine aside and talk to her about what Triple O had lined up for her.

"Oh, Catherine, I was looking for you to ask you something."

"What girl," Catherine said with an attitude.

"I just need to tell you something important, can you come to my room?" Sanity tried to whisper so that no one else could hear her.

Catherine walked to Sanity's room and they both sat on the side of Sanity's bed. Sanity wasted no time telling Catherine Triple O had some good plans for her. Catherine started smiling and told Sanity that it was good for her. "Sanity, so you really like music, don't you?"

"Yeah, I love it and that's what I'm telling you. Triple O was helping me record a song that I didn't get to finish because we were sneaking over there. We didn't have a lot of time to do it, but now he has a photo shoot lined up for me uptown this weekend and he also wants me to finish the song so that he can put my photos on my album cover."

"Oh my God are you for real?" Catherine asked.

"Yes, I'm for real. So are you going to let me do it?"

"Yes, you know I'm going to let you do it. I told you to just let me know whenever you go so that

I can go with you. What day does he want you to do all of this?"

"Tomorrow. He wants me to come and finish the song and the next day he wants me to be uptown to do the shoot."

"Okay so we can go around there tomorrow and just let me know what time and I will just make everybody think we are just walking around the block, so I hope it don't take too long."

"Okay it won't because we were almost done. I only had one more track to work on," Sanity said feeling overly excited.

Eight o'clock the next day Sanity and Catherine walked to Triple O's house to finish her song. As soon as Triple O opened his door, he looked like he saw a ghost because the last conversation he had with Sanity was when she left out of there scared out of her mind. Catherine wasn't supposed to know that her and Tim were recording in his studio, so it was a shock to him to see Sanity's mother with her with a smile on her face as big as Sanity's.

Triple O yelled out, "now that's what I'm talking about! Momma here tonight so I know you're going to show out right?" He asked Sanity.

Sanity laughed and said, "I don't know I will see." It took them about an hour to put the last finishing touches on the song. Catherine started asking Triple O how long her daughter and son were coming to the studio and how he met them. At that point Sanity really didn't care what Catherine knew; all she knew was that Catherine was on board with her and what she wanted to do. Triple O told

Catherine exactly how he met them and how long he'd known them. Catherine then told Triple O how proud she was of Sanity. Hearing those words from Catherine did not touch Sanity's heart because there was a disconnect there. Sanity had never heard that before from their mother, so she started to wonder why now. But that was just another conversation that went in one of Sanity's ears and out the other, a conversation she cared nothing about.

It was time for Sanity's photo shoot and Catherine seemed more excited about it then Sanity did. Since Catherine was so great at doing hair, she made sure Sanity's hair was prettier than it had ever been before. Sanity did not know how to feel about that as well. It was a good thing Keisha was born with such a blessed talent for doing hair, so she made sure she kept the latest hair styles out. Sanity was feeling the moment and didn't let her feelings show or mind wondered. All she knew was that her life was taking a turn for the better.

Sanity and Catherine took a taxi uptown to do the photo shoot. When they arrived, Sanity was in shock and couldn't believe her dreams were finally coming true and her mom was at least acting like she was proud of her. She just didn't know if she should have been excited about Catherine being a part of her dreams or to prepare herself for what was coming next. It was very strange Catherine was all for Sanity's passion for acting and music all of a sudden. Sanity brushed the thought of Catherine's actions and interests in her off as another one of her fraudulent tricks for trades. When the photographer came out to meet with Sanity, Catherine started fixing her hair up, making sure her makeup was freshly done while introducing herself as Sanity's mother and biggest support system, which was not true at all. She made sure she would turn Sanity into a joke and embarrass her in front of any kind of company.

Sanity felt she was always the desert at the dinner table in her head, meaning after any and everybody were talked about then the topic jumped on her with Catherine starting the conversation. She couldn't remember one time when the conversation was positive when speaking about her. Catherine joked about Sanity's dreams more than often; she even told Sanity to stop trying to chase dead end dreams because she was too young, and no one would even take the time out to focus on a kid's career. Of course, that shattered Sanity and even though Willie wasn't aware of what Sanity was into, she always remembered he told her she could do anything she wanted to do.

After Catherine signed the paperwork for Sanity giving the photographer permission to take the photos, she looked at Sanity and said, "how are you feeling?"

Sanity said, "I'm good. I'm just ready to go." Catherine wondered why Sanity's mood changed, little did Catherine know her being there didn't sit well with Sanity because she felt the support was fake. After the shoot was over the photograph shook Sanity and Catherine's hand letting them know that Sanity did a great job with her poses. Catherine asked him if he had a number or a business card to be contacted and she also told him from that point on he would have to reach out to her with any information or questions concerning Sanity.

After the taxi arrived to pick them back up Sanity asked Catherine if it was okay for her to spend the weekend with her cousin because she was still excited about doing the shoot and wanted to tell her cousin. "No, because I need you to go somewhere with me tomorrow morning." Sanity thought it was a favor for a favor and the time had come for Sanity to finally say no to Catherine.

"Catherine, I don't feel like going anywhere tomorrow. I just wanted to go spend time with my cousin! Where do you need me to go with you?" She turned towards the window and rolled her eyes with a disgusted look on her face.

"Now Sanity why you asking me something so crazy? You already know where I want you to go with me. But you know what? Don't even worry about it see that's why I don't let your ass go anywhere now." At that point Sanity just stayed quiet so that she wouldn't end up saying something she would have regretted. Catherine went on and on in Sanity's ear. Sanity remained quiet as a mouse.

Chapter 31

Things got really rough for Sanity in school because she was spending most of her nights recording in the studio. She tried to continue going to school but things got really hectic for her between both. The more hours Willie worked gave Sanity the lead way to spend more time at the studio and that's what she did every chance she got. Catherine didn't tell Willie anything about Sanity and the music. She still had an attitude with Sanity for not agreeing to go with her to see her mistress at the prison and no matter how much she tried to hide it Sanity saw the way Catherine would look at her when she would walk through the house. The older Sanity got the more she developed her own thoughts about life and death.

During Sanity's high school years, her body was developing into a woman. Her hips were spreading, and she knew it, but the one thing Sanity hated about herself was not being able to keep her composure around a crowd of people, mainly men. Things changed for Sanity after a few weekends of going to the prison with Catherine. It turned Sanity against a lot of things that were supposed to have been normal in life. Sanity had missed so many days out of school for not going, being suspended, and asked to return with a parent. However, Catherine would not follow the school guidelines by bringing Sanity back so that she could have a parent teacher conference. Most of the time Sanity got suspended, it was told that she could return with a parent. There were times when Sanity and her siblings got suspended until a parent brought them back and believe it or not, they would be out of school for days. Catherine had every excuse in the book to why she couldn't take them back each day that passed by. She always failed to tell Willie the kids were able to go back to school if a parent brought them back. This was because she knew she would have to take them back.

Willie truly believed in all of his kids getting a good education he stayed on their backs about school if nothing else. Sanity had gotten suspended so much from school for skipping class until she went to school her junior year. She had to go to the office to get her class schedule and when she got there the office was packed but that was the norm for the first week of school. Following a class schedule wasn't the easiest thing to do because most of the time the schedules were out of order. This made the first week of school always the most hectic. Sanity had anxiety attacks here and there, but she was not the type to tell anyone how she was feeling inside.

High school wasn't Sanity's first time feeling that way. During middle school, anytime she was around a large crowd and older guys, it would cause her heart to beat fast, triggering an anxiety attack. Sanity was sitting in the office waiting in the corner to be called next for her class schedule. She had gotten even more nervous the longer she waited. "Miss Sanity Nova," the guidance counselor yelled. Sanity was excited and nervous all at once because she knew she was coming close to graduating in a year.

"Yes, right here," Sanity yelled as she was waving her hand from side to side. The guidance counselor signaled her to follow her to the office. Sanity really got nervous then because there were only a few students that were called in the office. Sanity was puzzled as to why she closed the door.

As Sanity was sitting in the guidance counselor office with the door closed waiting for her to return with her schedule, she started praying to herself. She just didn't know what to pray for; all she knew was something wasn't right. The counselor returned with a big smile on her face, a note in her hand, and a weird class schedule for Sanity. She looked down at Sanity and said, "we are giving you another chance to get this school thing right so I'm expecting you to do the right thing this year Miss Nova do you understand me?"

"Yes, I do but why are we walking all the way back here. Did they change grade halls this year or something?"

The counselor stopped in her tracts, "wait what Sanity? So you didn't know you were on the list for alternative school this year because of all your write ups, suspension and absentees."

"No, I didn't know. No one said anything to me. Did my parents know that I would have to attend an alternative school this year?" Sanity felt her throat closing in on her because she wanted to break down right then and there.

"Well, I called and spoke to your mother and she told me she would let you know, and we also mailed out several notices over the summer break letting all of your parents know." This was just another one of those conversations that went over Catherine's head because she didn't tell anyone, not even Sanity and she was the one that needed the heads up before school began.

Sanity got to her first period class and realized her best friend Jada was already sitting in the class. As soon as she opened the door, they locked eyes, and burst out laughing at each other because they felt like it was their rules their way. They made a pact that nothing or no one could ever tear them apart. Her best friend Jada was smiling. Sanity tried to walk to the back of the class to sit next to Jada, but the teacher stopped that real quick. "Not this year. Y'all will not run me crazy."

Jada was the type to pop off really quick, so she asked the teacher, "what do you mean? You don't even know us so why would you say that?"

The teacher replied, "you think I don't know y'all? Trust me I do."

"Oh so what that's what y'all do, talk about y'all students to each other around here?" That was a surreal moment for Sanity. Their school records from the time they started had been passed on to the alternative school giving them the impression that Sanity and Jada were always in trouble for skipping classes and that's what every teacher believed. For Sanity, things were a little different because she had a guidance counselor that really cared about her actions and she really wanted to know how she could have helped Sanity during school and outside of school.

"Oh no, Sanity get right back up here to the front of the class. You guys will not sit together in my class," the teacher said. I was told to separate y'all two because there will be no clowning this year in this class." Sanity wasn't the type to talk back, if anything she was embarrassed from being put on the spot in front of the whole class. She didn't respond, she just did what the teacher asked her to. As Sanity sat down in her assigned seat, she got her social studies book out. She heard a very slow deep tone of voice at the door asking the teacher if he was in the right class. "What's your name," she asked the medium height light brown young man.

"My name is Michael Pearson, but they call me Mike!"

"Okay yes Michael you are in the right place and we are going over the warm-up assignment, so you can just grab a seat anywhere." Michael walked to the back of the class to sit down and as soon as he sat down, he raised his hand to let the teacher know that for some reason he didn't get a book for her class.

"Okay no problem Mike you can come up here and share a book with Sanity."

"Huh," Sanity said out loud, causing Jada to laugh.

"What do you mean huh? Sanity I already told you and your little laughing best friend back there that I'm not doing this with y'all this year." Sanity had a way with words everyone loved when she came around because she was so blunt when she said something, she meant it.

"What I didn't even mean nothing by it I just said huh dang," Sanity said.

"That's what I thought and for you little lady you can look forward to me staying on your back this year" the teacher replied. "Because I see a lot of potential in you. You just have to believe it but we are not going to talk about that right now during class. Miss Nova just know I got my eyes on you."

Mike sat next to Sanity looking just as shy as she was then he introduced himself again to her, "hi Sanity." This was the closest Sanity had been to a guy she knew nothing about. Her anxiety tried to kick in, but she said a silent prayer and things felt better. Sanity felt a moment of relief until Michael passed his number to her without anyone seeing. Sanity took it with a smile on her face. As Sanity made her way out the door of the classroom once class ended, she threw Michael's number in the small trash can.

Sanity waited for Jada outside of the classroom so that they could walk to their next class together.

"Girl what in the hell are we doing here," Sanity said to Jada.

"Man, I don't know but don't trip girl it's so many people here that we know but the thing I don't like about it is that we are all mixed in with other small county schools and I'm sure we don't know any of them folks."

"What do you mean other counties? Girl, how do you know all of this," Sanity asked Jada.

"Shit one of my older female cousins brought me to the conference after they sent out about ten damn letters to the house about it."

"Oh my God, so they did reach out to our parents about this?"

"Yeah Sanity where you been girl? When I tell you they stayed sending those letters out over the summer break."

"Girl you know Cat go mute in certain situations and I guess this was one of them because Willie doesn't even know I got kicked out of school." She shook her head, slowly quickly jumping on another subject because she felt herself getting angry all over again.

"Hey hey." There was that same familiar voice as Sanity and Jada were laughing. Sanity said to herself what does this boy want now? Both Sanity and Jada turned around because she knew it was Michael trying to get her attention. It wasn't that she wasn't so interested in him, it's just that she knew her life was a secret mess. Sanity wasn't the type to deal with boys at this point in her life. She was too busy focusing on a way out.

"Yeah," she said to Michael with a very shy voice. Sanity nudged Jada and told her to hush before Michael got close enough to hear them.

"Girl stop. Don't make that boy feel bad he might think we are talking bad about him."

"No, I hope he doesn't because I'm laughing at you not him."

"Why are you laughing at me? I ain't say nothing funny."

"No but you look scared as heck. I really wish you could see yourself right now because it's showing all over your face," Jada said as she continued to laugh at Sanity. "So shut up. Stop before he gets close," Sanity said, "and I start laughing in his face for no reason just because you're laughing."

When Michael made his way close to Sanity and Jada, he stood close, looked her right in her full eyes and said, "you must have forgotten something." Sanity told him no she didn't think so because she really was puzzled with his question. "Yes, you did," he replied.

Sanity smiled and said, "what?" She really thought he was joking with her, but it turned out that Michael watched Sanity throw his number in the trash can and he waited until she walked out of the classroom to search for it. Michael reached in his pocket and pulled out the same paper he gave Sanity with his name and number on it.

"Oh my God Sanity," said with both hands over her mouth feeling so ashamed because she got caught up. "I'm so sorry. I meant no harm by that I just didn't know what to say to you if I did decide to call." Michael chuckled a little and asked Sanity what she meant by that. "I mean I have never dated before," Sanity said. "For the most part, I hang with dudes, not date them."

"I know. I see you and all your lil friends like hanging with the dudes huh?"

"Yes, we do. They are like our brothers. They protect us," Jada added to their conversation with a little frustrated tone. It was like every time someone brought up the fact that they hung out with dudes as friends, Jada took offense. Sanity didn't let small talk bother her too much because she believed people choose their path to love. Sanity knew Jada felt the same way as she did about it. It's just that Jada wasn't the one to spread rumors or assume anything other than the truth about her.

"Okay I'm sorry," Sanity said to Michael. "If you're not mad at me as a matter of fact, here's my number. Call me when we get out of school."

"Okay I gotcha just make sure you don't accidentally throw my number away again," Michael said as he walked away and laughed. Sanity and Jada watched Michael walk away and they both thought he was cute and dressed really nice, but again Sanity's mind was far from a man. All she wanted was to live her dream life.

Things moved quickly with Sanity and Michael. They thought they were so in love as the time went by. Sanity was at school with one of her very close cousins and the date had come for Sanity's monthly doctor appointment. Her cousin walked over to the alternative campus and whispered, "Sanity cousin, do you need a ride so that I could take you to the clinic to get your birth control shot?"

"Oh, heck yeah please do," Sanity said. The school day came to an end and Sanity, her cousins, and Jada hopped in Sanity's cousin's old school two door car to drive up the street to the neighborhood clinic. It was only a block away from their high school campus. Once they arrived, they joked about every girl in there being pregnant. Once Sanity's cousin was done with her appointment, they called Sanity back for a urine sample. The first thing Sanity said to the clinical receptionist was, "hey how are you doing today?"

"I'm great," the woman replied with a big smile on her face. It seemed like she was having a great day that day. The next few words that she said to Sanity were, "Congratulations Sanity you are pregnant!" Sanity knew something was wrong because she slept entirely too much.

Not one time did Catherine come to her to talk about anything that may have been suspicious. Instead, she made everyone think the worst of the facts. To Sanity it was just another way to paint her bad in everyone's eyes because Sanity had put a stop to her secret weekend runs with Catherine. Sanity felt as if Catherine developed a feeling of tension and hate towards her. Sanity knew too much about her secret love triangle.

When Sanity and her cousin arrived at Sanity's house, they tried to come up with a way to hide the fact that Sanity was pregnant, but they realized there was no way to get around that. Sanity and her cousin sat in her cousin's car at the top of the street to get prepared for what everyone was going to say. Years earlier Catherine thought it was cool to tell certain family members that she thought Sanity was gay from another one of her crazy assumptions about Sanity and the craziest thing was all of the children were so over the way Catherine acted. Sanity knew in her heart all of her siblings were not at ease, but she was too young herself to make a difference for all of them. She barely held her own feelings together. She broke down in silence, many days without anyone knowing at all. Once she would cry her eyes out it made her feel a little better about life, but the pain was still there.

Once Sanity's cousin pulled in front of the house, she looked at Sanity and said, "alright cousin I'm about to go! Are you going to be okay?"

"Yes, cousin I am. I'm just so scared of what Willie might say. I know he's going to be mad at me. I know that for sure."

"Sanity you're saying Willie is going to be mad, hell what about Catherine? Because you know she ain't right," as she rolled her eyes and looked away with an attitude. Sanity just laughed.

She said, "you know what I'm seventeen now and it can't be too bad or too much for them to be ashamed of. Now the only thing that's got me scared is what if they put me out? I have nowhere to go because ain't nobody letting a young pregnant girl live in their house with nothing going on for herself but a prayer and a dream!"

"Girl it will be fine, just go in there and tell them what's going on they may be happy who knows."

"Naw I doubt that but okay I will see you tomorrow at school if I don't get killed tonight by Willie. I don't think Catherine care at all you see she didn't even tell me anything about being kicked out of school. She let me get right up for school looking stupid. I wonder if she even fought for me when they called her and told her the decision was made for me not to return the following school year?"

Sanity got out of the car with all of her emotions running high not knowing what she was up against. All she knew was that she probably would have never been looked at the same once she tells them she was pregnant. She was okay with Catherine's family knowing but the last thing she wanted to do was disappoint her other grandmother. Willie's mother showed all of her grandkids the same amount of love and it hurt Sanity more to tell her than it did to tell Catherine's side of the family. Willie's mother made sure she placed the words of God on their hearts from birth and Sanity didn't want to be looked at a certain way because she had gone out and got pregnant at such a young age without being married. Sanity turned to her cousin Tiesha and said, "forget this I'm just going to go in here and wait on Catherine to say something to me. If she doesn't say anything then I'm not gonna say anything. I'm just gonna act like I took the birth control shot today and that's it."

"Well cousin, just do what you think you should do," Tiesha said. Sanity walked in the house scared out of her mind. She was more scared of what Willie would say than anyone because he couldn't stand the thought of anyone even speaking bad about any of his kids. As Sanity walked past Catherine's room, she could see her moving around fixing up her area where she would do her hair all the time. Sanity then heard Catherine calling her name.

"Sanity, Sanity come here now!" Catherine yelled. Sanity made her way back down the hall to Catherine's room. When she got to the door, Catherine turned towards her away from the mirror. She took one look at Sanity and said, "what did that doctor say today?" Before Sanity could respond Catherine yelled out as loud as she could for Big Mamma to come to her room. "Big Mamma this damn girl done went out and got pregnant! Sanity, I know your ass pregnant." Catherine said, "girl your life is over, you will never be shit now, how the hell are you going to take care of a damn baby and go to school? Because I know one thing, I'm not watching no damn baby. You made your bed, so you have to lay in it." Only one thing that Catherine said registered to Sanity, and it was that she made her bed so she would have to lay in it. The reason that stuck to Sanity was because it was one of Big Mamma's ways of telling you that if you did something wrong you would have to face whatever consequences come behind it. So those weren't the words of Catherine. She repeated Big Mamma's words.

Once she got to Catherine's door, she looked at Sanity crying and said, "what's wrong with you gal?" Even though Sanity was pregnant, she felt horrible because Catherine didn't give her a chance to say anything; She assumed, although correctly. Sanity was already beating herself up about it and just didn't think Catherine would have said anything in the nature of which she did.

"I'm pregnant Big Mamma!" Sanity said, "I already know I will never be nothing." She walked off to her room crying still even more afraid of what Willie would say when he got in from work. Surprisingly, when Willie arrived later that afternoon no one said anything to him about Sanity being pregnant. A few days had passed by and Sanity met some school friends at the bus stop. She tried to cover up the fact that she was pregnant, but the shame was so noticeable to everyone that even the bus driver asked her if she was okay. By the time they arrived at school, Sanity felt like all eyes were on her.

"Omg Sanity," said to her best friend Jada. "What are you okay?"

"Yeah girl, but I feel like everyone is looking at me," Sanity whispered to Jada.

"Girl you are tripping. Ain't nobody looking at you," Jada said as she fell to the ground laughing as hard as she could. That made Sanity feel so much better and realized that it was just her mind wondering. During that week of school, there was an audition going on and a few of the students knew that Sanity was singing for her brother Tim and a few of his friends in the hood. The teacher played a song by Kirk Franklin and asked Sanity if she could sing the female version of the song. Since the teacher saw so much good in her, she agreed to performing the song for the class. After Sanity performed, she felt a sense of relief because she was able to put being pregnant aside for a few minutes. As soon as the bell rang, Sanity, Jada, and Michael walked out of class and heard the teacher call Sanity's name. Sanity told Jada and Michael to wait a few seconds while she sees what the teacher wanted.

"Sanity, I heard something, and I need you to tell me the truth, okay?" The teacher said.

"Yeah okay. What is it," Sanity asked.

"Well, I've been hearing some talk around here that you're about to be a mom."

Sanity started crying and said, "yes and I know I'm young, and I also know that my life will change. I have heard it all from my mom."

The teacher then took a deep breath and said, "yes! Your life will definitely change but you don't have to go through this alone. I am always here for you and your baby Sanity. Now I won't promise you that it will be easy but what I can promise you is that we will get through this together if you allow me to be there." That caused Sanity to cry even more because Catherine made her feel like her life had come to an end and Sanity's teacher made her feel like she could be loved the way she wanted her mom to love her.

Sanity hugged her teacher so tight as she cried and told her thank you for always staying on her and being there. When Sanity walked back out of the class to meet back up with Jada and Michael, they noticed her eyes were red and puffy.

"Aw babes what's wrong," Michael asked Sanity. There was no way to hide the pregnancy any longer, so with Jada standing right there she walked away slowly.

She looked back at Michael and said, "it seems like everyone knows so we should just tell everyone," as she threw her hand up in frustration.

Jada was so confused she looked at Sanity and said, "what are you talking about? Tell what?"

"I'm pregnant friend. I'm pregnant," Sanity yelled out while Michael just stood there looking puzzled as if he had no clue.

"Oh wow, really Sanity? I knew something was wrong with you," Jada said.

"Well yeah that's what it is," Sanity replied. Michael turned to walk back towards Sanity with the same puzzled look. He told Sanity that he may have told a few of the wrong people and he was sorry. Sanity immediately got upset with Michael and told him that she prays he was ready for what Willie may have to say if he had to hear it from someone in the town and not them himself. After a few days of Willie not knowing and Catherine walking around the house not speaking to Sanity but giving her disgusting looks, Willie stormed into Sanity's room with a surprising look on his face. He said, "so Sanity I know this is not true what your mother just told me. You didn't let some boy get you knocked up huh?"

Sanity looked at Willie and said, "yes Willie I accidentally got pregnant!"

Willie dropped his head and said, "Sanity hear me and hear me well. It ain't no such thing that you accidentally got pregnant. Getting pregnant is not an accident, you knew exactly what you were doing baby." Sanity just sat there quietly because she realized that her father was telling God's honest truth.

"Willie, I know but I didn't mean to do this," Sanity said as she was crying hysterically because she was more embarrassed and worried about what her dad's side of the family would have thought of her than being a young mom.

As the time went by, school became a nightmare for Sanity. Her belly started growing fast and it was becoming too much for her to hide it. She was quick to tell anyone "no" that asked if she was having a child. It became too obvious to everyone because her weight started changing by the weeks. After waking up one morning for school, Willie told her to catch a taxi and he would pay for it. She became sick from her pregnancy and was late every day. School was the last thing on her mind, she just wanted to get through her pregnancy stress and be pain free, so she dropped out. Of course, she felt like a loser especially after Catherine had already told her that she would never be anything due to her getting pregnant at such a young age. As the time went by, before she knew it, she was weeks away from being a young mother and having someone that would depend on her for everything and someone that would love her unconditionally.

Sanity started walking around the neighborhood every day for at least thirty minutes because Big Mamma told her that would make labor and delivery much easier, so she did whatever Big Mamma told her to do when it came to being a first-time young mother.

"Yo, Sanity I haven't seen you in a while. Tim told me you were pregnant," Triple O said as he was walking past Sanity to the local neighborhood store. "Sanity you sneaky as hell because no one even knew you had a boyfriend," he laughed.

Sanity laughed along with him and said, "yeah I know, and I know a lot of people are looking down on me right now because I'm young and pregnant. I just try to stay in the house a lot so that I won't be seen. That way no one would have much to say about me. Triple O started feeling sorry for Sanity, it was all in his eyes.

He said, "Sanity it's plenty of young girls pregnant right now like you, so you shouldn't feel bad at all about bringing your own personal problems into this world." Since Triple O was much older, he spoke a little knowledge to both Sanity and Tim. When Sanity made it back from her daily walk, she stopped at the bottom of the steps to catch her breath. As she lifted her head up to continue up the stairs, she noticed Catherine walked out the door. Catherine had left her first lover, Jimmy, alone. She had moved on to a younger guy that she met at Keisha's son's first birthday party. Keisha's son's father was related to a lot of people around town. His long-distance cousins were also in attendance at Keisha's son's party along with the many older cousins and one of the cousins that had done a few years in prison. Catherine had Sanity at her side the whole time during the party because that's where Sanity wanted to be. Because Keisha was so tied up with making sure her son had a great party, it made it hard for Sanity to hang out with her. She stood next to Catherine the entire time because Tim wasn't there. He came later that night to see his nephew and wish him a happy birthday. The older men stood around in the front yard drinking and telling jokes while the kids played in the backyard.

Somehow, Catherine made her way near the men, being all quiet and looking innocent to everyone, but it was a good thing any family from Catherine's side knew exactly what and who they were dealing with when it came to her. She could fool strangers, but as time went by several family members knew all about Catherine's lies and conniving attempts.

Sanity caught her breath and walked up the stairs. "Where are you going Catherine," she asked.

"Oh child. I'm grown and I wanted to talk to Michael about something too." Catherine said, "I just wanted to know since you're so close to having this baby. I wanted to know if he could stay here at the house with you just in case you get sick or go into labor and I'm not around." Sanity was happy to have her boyfriend there every day, but she was also broken at the same time because she really thought since she was so young and afraid of being a mom that Catherine would have to stand by her side that time through it all, but no. Sanity wasn't surprised, it was just what she expected. The time had come for Sanity to deliver her child and Catherine was out with her newfound love, which was the guy she met at her grandson's birthday party months prior. Big Mamma sat up all night beside Sanity's bed hoping and praying that she didn't go into labor with just the two of them there. She told Sanity that no matter what, she will have a good delivery even if she had to deliver the baby herself. Sanity was scared and excited because she felt alone. Michael didn't answer his phone, Willie was working overtime, and Catherine was out having a good time. Catherine made sure she told Sanity before she left earlier that day not to call her unless her water broke, and she was going into labor. So, Sanity didn't call her, and she didn't feel like she needed to because Big Mamma was right by her side the whole time.

The moment Big Mamma got up and walked to her room, Sanity screamed throughout the house that her water broke. Big Mamma went back to Sanity's room as fast as she could, and by the time she made it, Sanity stood there frightened. She told Big Mamma that she thought her water broke but she wasn't in any pain, so that eased Big Mamma's mind.

"Okay gal if you're not feeling any pain I'm going to go ahead and call Catherine and let her know she needs to get her butt back here to get you to the hospital right now." Big Mamma yelled at Catherine over the phone, "Hey Cat, this gal is in labor and you need to find a way back over here as soon as possible before I call the ambulance." "It don't make no sense she just leaves here knowing you could have this baby any day now," Big Mamma said in frustration. "She did this same thing when Keisha went in labor and she needs to learn that she's a grandma now and she needs to act like it." Then she went on to say, "she waited until she started getting grandkids, and now she's worse off than she was when y'all was younger. She should really be ashamed of herself. Got everybody thinking she such a good mother and don't care about nobody but herself."

As they waited for Catherine to arrive Sanity tried to call Michael but got no answer. After about thirty minutes of Big Mamma calling Catherine, a car

pulled up blowing the horn multiple times. It was
Catherine with her new lover's sister. They rushed
Sanity out of the house to the car and the first thing
Catherine said to Sanity was, "so you see now right?
Having these babies is no joke. I was out having a
good time. You sure know how to ruin somebody's
night!"

"Okay," Sanity said to Catherine. "You can
just go back to have fun y'all can just drop me off
since I'm not having any pain anyway." Sanity
wanted to cry so bad, but her unborn child wouldn't
let her. She wanted to stay as calm as possible
because Big Mamma always told her that whatever
she felt in her mind emotionally could affect her baby
as well. She thought about it while Catherine and her
new friend laughed and joked the whole way to the
hospital. It was very clear that the both of them were
out having a good time because you could smell the
alcohol and smoke on their clothes. Before Sanity
made it upstairs to the maternity ward, Michael
walked through the door in a very frantic mood.

"Hey, my girlfriend is here and she about to
have a baby," he yelled to the front desk receptionist.

"Michael I'm right here," Sanity yelled as she
walked towards the front desk. They rushed Sanity
upstairs to the maternity ward and before they knew
it, Sanity had strong pains in her back. That indicated
that she was really in labor. Sanity's labor lasted
nineteen hours which felt like forever to her because
the whole time she was in pain. Catherine sat at her
bedside badgering her about being a young mother
and how things would get worse for her in life.

Before she knew it, the doctors came in to check on Sanity's progress and it was time for her to give birth to one of the most blessed gifts she would have ever received.

After hours of hard labor and being put down, Sanity and Michael welcomed a handsome baby boy. Sanity took one look at her son and realized that no matter how hard things got for them, she would protect him from any pain that she had ever experienced in her life. Just a few days into being a new mom, Sanity had gotten so fed up with the treatment from Catherine. After the weekend, trips were finally over for Sanity. The emotional abuse became Catherine's way of dealing with Sanity. Tim came over to the house to see Sanity and his nephew. Sanity told Tim that she was so fed up with Catherine and her wicked ways. She told him that she felt it was best that she moved out with Michael because they needed to raise their own child without having Catherine put them down every day. She also said whenever Catherine walked past her room, she would see her playing with her baby and she acted as if he didn't exist. Sanity was already full of embarrassment because Catherine didn't show any interest in bonding with her grandson and that feeling was too familiar to Sanity.

"Sis I understand," Tim said as he helped Sanity pack all of her things. Sanity didn't tell anyone she was moving out and if Tim hadn't come by to see her, he wouldn't have known either. "Sanity you have to do what you got to do now sis. I'm not mad at you but that boy better treat you right," he said as he pointed to Sanity's face. Once Michael and his father pulled up, Tim ran to the door to signal them not to blow the horn because Big Mamma was in her room asleep and she didn't know Sanity was leaving as well. Tim helped Sanity move her things out as fast as they could and then Tim left to act as if he was never there.

Things got really rough for Sanity once she left home. She was living with Michael and his family. It was another situation where Sanity was living in an overcrowded house but what made it worse that time was the fact that Sanity had a little baby. To Sanity it was bad, but it was better than the treatment she got from Catherine. Sanity felt very weird. Two months later she held out on going to the doctor because it was time for another checkup after giving birth to her son. The day of her appointment she felt worse than she did when she went into labor with her son.

"Hi Sanity," the doctor said after his assistant had collected blood and urine from her. "So how are you feeling since the birth of this handsome little fella?"

"I'm doing okay," Sanity said. "I just been feeling really sick lately, but I think it's because I been barely eating since I gave birth to him."

"Well Sanity no and I think I know why you have been feeling the way you have been feeling. Sanity, you're pregnant again." The doctor knew that the news wasn't what Sanity expected to hear because her eyes immediately turned red from holding back her tears as long as she could. She not only had one little boy that depended on her, but some months later there would be two little humans that would be depending on her for everything.

Sanity said to the doctor, "oh no this can't be true. I just had him how can I have another child right now. What am I going to do?" The room got so silent all you could hear was Sanity praying out to God in a very soft scared voice.

"Sanity listen, you're not the first and you won't be the last," the doctor said to her. "This is your life, and you just have to do what you need to do as a mother now. This is not the end of the world or your life. You got time to give your kids a great life."

"I know," Sanity said. "I just don't know where to start. I'm already having a hard time and the only help I got with my son is both of his grandparents. My dad even tries to help out here and there, but he works long hours, and this is my child, so I know it's my job to take care of him. I just wish things were different for me," Sanity said with tears flowing down her face. Little did everyone know that she was going through pure hell with Michael and his dishonest ways.

Everyone in the town heard about Michael cheating on Sanity with multiple women. The rumors had even surfaced about a baby with another woman, but Sanity chumped it up and tried to come up with an escape plan for her and her son.

After hiding her second pregnancy from as many people as she could, she had applied for public housing the minute she knew she was expecting her first son in the same projects that Keisha lived in. She called day in and day out to check the status of her application and no matter how desperate she told the project manager she was. They didn't move her name any closer on the waiting list. Months passed by and Sanity was not any closer to moving into her own apartment and she began to lose faith along the way. One day, Sanity received a call from Catherine saying that she wanted to see her and the baby. Sanity was very hesitant about going back over to the hell hole that she freed herself from, but being the person she was, she decided to get her son dressed and put her on something that would disguise her pregnancy. She strapped her son into his stroller and she walked miles to see what Catherine wanted to talk about. She felt that when she got there Catherine would finally apologize for everything she put her through and exposed her to. When Sanity got there, she noticed a few of her aunts were there and some family friends.

"Hey Sanity, let me see that big handsome baby of yours," her aunt said as she started unstrapping the baby to hold him.

"Come here Sanity," she heard Catherine yell. At that moment, she realized there was no way her and Catherine were about to have a heart to heart if she was calling her in the next room to come and sit with her in a room full of people.

"Um, Catherine said. "So why the hell are you living over there with that boy with no power?"

"What are you talking about Cat," said Sanity. "So that's what you wanted me to come over here for?" Sanity covered her mouth and laughed to keep from crying from humiliation. Sanity looked

Catherine in the eyes because that was the moment that took her to a place she never wanted to go with her again. It reminded her of the times she went to the prison with Catherine and when she first started looking at Catherine in the worst way a child could ever look at her own mother. Sanity thought somewhere in the back of her little mind that Catherine would have been done with her abuse she caused over the years. Catherine seemed to be unstoppable and had gotten worse over the years, but not once did she apologize to Sanity when she arrived to see her at her request. However, she was still up to her no-good spirit breaking ways.

The question of "are you pregnant again" kept coming up at Sanity. The more she was faced with that question, the more she became determined to be the best mom that she could be to her children. Sanity always told everyone that it wasn't true that she was expecting another child so soon after her first son.

"Hello Sanity Nova," a voice spoke through sanity's prepaid cell phone.

"Yes, hi this is Sanity speaking," she said back to the lady over the phone.

"Well Sanity I have some great news for you. Your name came up next on our waiting list for a two-bedroom one bathroom apartment and we want to know are you still interested?"

"Yes of course," Sanity said. "Yes, I been waiting on this call for the longest. What do I need to do?" Sanity was so excited about the call she didn't tell anyone right away but the first person who did find out was Tim because he made sure no matter where Sanity was, he would come and check on her and her son. It was a week since Sanity had gotten the call to move into her first apartment when Tim came walking up the street to see her sitting on the porch with her son.

"Tim," Sanity said while she was feeling as if God blessed her with a new beginning. "I got some good news today. I'm finally moving into my own place!"

Tim said, "yo sis that's good now. You ain't gotta worry about nothing. You can finally focus on them babies first and then we can get back to the music and acting stuff."

"You're so right. I miss it so much," Sanity said. "It's just so hard right now with this baby." She tried to dismiss what Tim said when he mentioned taking care of those babies early on in their conversation.

"Naw," Tim said with a straight look on his face.

"What Tim, what you mean naw?"

"I mean you ain't got to keep lying to me. Sis I know you're pregnant again. Trust me the streets are talking and you're not the only one pregnant by this man either and I know you know that too." All their lives Sanity had told Tim the truth but that seemed to be another hard conversation to have with him just like what Catherine had put her through.

"Tim look, I really don't know what you're talking about, but I will say something to him about it when he gets home today." Sanity said, "Tim just have it."

"Look Sanity you can sit here and play crazy all you want to but everybody around town knows you're going through hell with this boy and you're playing yourself right now, for real sis!"

"Okay Tim if you say so," Sanity replied.

"Well, you're my sister," Tim said. "And I'm going to go with what you said but just know I'm not going to play stupid or blind."

The conversation jumped back on Sanity and her first apartment. "I'm so happy for you girl," Tim said. "Did you tell Big Mamma or anybody yet?"

"Well, I only told Willie so far. I told him not to tell anyone until I move all the way in, and he was so happy for me. He just told me that he had heard about the stuff you're saying that you heard about Michael, so I try not to stay on the phone with him too long."

"Yeah, we are grown in our eyes, but we are definitely still his little babies." They both laughed and mocked some of Willie's favorite words when he would fuss at them.

"That man crazy as hell Sanity but he loves us to death."

"Heck yeah that man will lay his life on the line for any of us. Boy we had hell growing up in that house," Sanity said to Tim. She laughed so hard until her son busted out in laughter as if he knew what they were laughing at.

Sanity finally moved into her place and had accepted the fact that she was soon to be a mom to two children. She needed to press forward to give them a way better life from what she was accustomed to. Sanity decided that when she moved into her first apartment, she would let Michael move in with her and her son because she was expecting her second kid and she did not want to go through it alone. She didn't want her sons to grow up in a single parent home so she did everything she could to hold her family together for the sake of them. Even when Michael constantly reminded her that her own mother was against her, there were times Michael would come home and tell Sanity that he saw her mother and how bad she talked about her for no reason. Sanity had several friends at the time that would also tell her how bad Catherine spoke about all of her children, but she had it out for Sanity for some reason.

One of Sanity's friends from school also lived in the projects that she had recently moved to. Most of Sanity's news came from the friend she knew along with everyone's business in the hood. She even had connections with Catherine's new boyfriend at the time so that was how Sanity heard of the nasty things that her mother had spread in the streets about all of her children. Sanity had come to the conclusion that Catherine was sick mentally.

Bonding with kids while they're still in the womb is the best form of bonding. Sanity just could not figure out what was going on inside of Catherine's head when she spoke badly of the kids that God had blessed her with. After many verbal fights and lonely nights inside of Sanity's apartment, she wanted to reach out to her big sister Keisha. She wanted to finally tell her what she had endured for many weekends with Catherine, especially when she would tell her that she could tag along. Sanity still didn't want anyone to know that she was about to give birth to another child, so she stayed in her apartment all day. If she needed to go anywhere, she made sure she covered up well enough that in case she did run into Keisha or any other family member they wouldn't be able to tell that she was pregnant again.

Tim made sure he didn't mention anything about Sanity's pregnancy to anyone, not even his closest friend because he felt bad for Sanity when people would talk about her being pregnant and being cheating on repeatedly. Sanity even worked at a call center during her second pregnancy. She was determined to prove Catherine wrong about how her life would turn out. She worked overtime every chance she got to try and to save up enough money to support her and two children. She then turned to the system for assistance. Michael came in whenever he wanted to and for the most part, he ignored Sanity's needs for him to be at home with her son while she at least made a way for them.

Things had gotten overwhelming for Sanity, so she decided to do what she had to do. She applied for assistance and got approved with the conditions of Michael going on child support to be forced to take care of her son. Sanity did not hesitate to move forward with the process. Deep down inside she really didn't want to put Michael on child support because she watched her dad work so hard to support them and she wanted to set that same example for her own children. But needless to say, Sanity made the best decision for her kids. One day Sanity prayed to God for a break-through and in the midst of her prayer a knock came to the door. It was the sheriff to serve Michael with papers for child support. Sanity acted like she didn't have a clue what was going on, but she didn't hold back anything when Michael tried to fight with her about it. She told him that he wasn't doing what he was supposed to for his son, and she had had enough of him and his selfish behavior.

"All you care about is what's outside of this house," Sanity said, screaming at Michael. "But when it comes to your child you see nothing and he's not a baby doll he is real, and he requires real love, care, and attention neither of those you give him! And I'm tired you see us struggling and you do nothing about it but yet still you're out here running around with all of these girls. Michael, you have a responsibility. Did you forget our dumb asses planned him?"

Michael's response to Sanity was always the same, he would smile, look at her, and say, "girl you will be alright," as he would turn to walk out the door. Sanity was in pain late that night after she had received a disturbing call that Michael had fathered a second child outside of her second pregnancy.

"Oh my God I'm bleeding," Sanity yelled knowing that no one was there but her and her son. Sanity had no choice but to make it to her apartment door to yell for help. One of Tim's friends walked to her door to check on her. She then yelled and told him to go run over to her sister Keisha's house and tell her son's father that she needed a ride up the street. So, he came about five minutes later, and he blew his horn for Sanity to come out. Sanity left her son with Tim's friend. She trusted him just as much as Tim did and he stayed checking on them every other day. Sanity ran to the car in excruciating pain, something she had never felt. She got in the car and screamed, "drive please drive! I'm about to have my baby oh God help me. I don't want to have this baby in your car!"

"Wait what," Keisha's boyfriend said. "Oh my God so you been prego this whole time? What you mean you about to have a baby?" Sanity screamed the entire way to the hospital.

"Let me out right here," Sanity said as soon as they pulled into the emergency entrance. Sanity walked into the hospital still in a lot of pain. She called Michael to let him know that she was in labor. When Michael answered he said, "go ahead. I will be up there later. I was there when you had the first one. Why do I have to be there now?" Sanity hung up. By the time they got her up to the maternity ward she was minutes away from pushing and Keisha ran in the room.

Keisha grabbed Sanity's hand and said, "Sanity it's going to be okay! But you have got to do what the doctor says. So push Sanity, push hard it's almost over." For the first time Sanity could see how much her pain affected Keisha as well because her eyes were full of tears. She held Sanity's hands as tight as she could, begging her to push so the pain would end.

"Sanity, congratulations you have a beautiful baby boy!" Sanity started crying because she knew in her heart that things would change with another child. She was left to care for two children all on her own because Michael made it very clear and noticeable that he wasn't ready to be a father to two children. He wanted to still do what high school kids did but Sanity was forced to grow up fast because of her upbringing.

She knew what disappointments to kids felt like all too well and she never wanted her sons to experience that kind of hurt. Sanity drifted off to sleep after she delivered her second son. She woke up to Willie who stood at her bedside holding her son smiling. As soon as he saw that Sanity was awake, he leaned over and gave her the biggest kid kiss on her forehead as he always did. He never changed the way he felt about his kids even though he and Catherine had a bad ending relationship.

"Aww my baby done had another baby," Willie said to Sanity.

"Yeah Willie, but I'm definitely not a baby anymore," Sanity said with a big smile on her face. "I guess you say your baby steady having babies."

"No girl, it's life," Willie said. "Just know these babies cost a lot of money so you are going to have to keep a job to support them, but you know no matter what daddy got you. You hear me Sanity?"

"Yes Willie. I know all of that already even you got my back because you always have had our backs."

Chapter 32

Sanity and Michael had been arguing all day about Michael's disrespectful behavior. Sanity worked extra hours to support her sons that Michael would have the same women he cheated with in her apartment for hours pretending that they were babysitting her sons. Sanity had gotten the information from the sister of one of his side girlfriends. At that point, Sanity had enough of Michael's lies and mistreatment, so she told him she wanted nothing else to do with him. He had been gone all day only for the power company to pay a visit to their home to disconnect the electricity. This was after he told Sanity not to worry about the bill because he paid it earlier that week. It was the week Sanity had to stay home with the kids because one of them didn't feel well. She took a few days off which caused her paycheck to be small. It wasn't enough to cover everything she needed to. Sanity slept a few nights in the dark cold house with her kids. By the fourth night of having bad nightmares and feeling something wasn't right in her spirit she decided to walk with her kids across the breezeway. She made her way to Keisha's place to stay a few nights until she could figure out something for her and her kids.

"What's up girl," Keisha said to Sanity.

"Nothing. I'm just so sick of this sorry ass man. He don't do nothing for these kids but he's around here making more babies. I'm tired and all he does is lie. Every time we approach the girl he tells them to their face it ain't true and they are so scared of him. They either walk away or say what he wants them to say then the sad part is they will wait until they get home to call my phone or text me giving me all of their nasty bedroom details. Keisha I'm just so sick of it," Sanity yelled.

"Sanity I heard it all, but I wasn't going to keep coming to you telling you stuff to hurt you because if I knew then I knew that you knew about it as well. That's your personal life so you need to move on for you and your kids because yes I have heard of a few people he's dealing with and you know them too."

Sanity looked at her kids and at Keisha and said, "I can't lie my mind been off and all over the place all night, besides I just needed to leave the house for a day or two." Sanity and Keisha had a few words later that night because Sanity's children would not stop crying. As soon as Sanity got both of her kids to sleep, she went to sleep with one of them at the foot of Keisha's front room couch. Sanity tossed and turned all night and she tried her best not to wake her babies. "Sanity, Sanity, oh my God!"

Keisha ran into the front room crying and screaming, "please get up please oh God!"

"What girl, what's wrong with you," she jumped up as fast as she could. "Keisha talk to me, what is going on?"

"Sanity please come here," Keisha screamed and grabbed her as tight as she could.

"What happened?" Sanity started yelling, "tell me what's wrong with you?"

"Tim is dead!" Keisha yelled and in that very moment Sanity's whole life turned upside down in the blink of an eye. Sanity screamed and asked Keisha what she was talking about. She even started trying to fight with Keisha because her mind started thinking crazy, so she assumed that because her and Keisha had a disagreement before they went to bed that somehow this was Keisha's way of getting back at her.

"No Sanity it's true," Keisha said while she was crying holding Sanity as tight as she could making sure she didn't lose it completely. "It really is true; they said the highway patrolman found his body on the side of the road this morning, but it looked like he was out there all night alone." All Sanity kept saying to Keisha was that the horrible phone call that she had just received about Tim was a lie and somehow someone was playing tricks on them. Sanity did not believe one word that came out of Keisha's mouth.

"Keisha, who called you? Who the hell told you this? I need to talk to them myself," Sanity repeated over and over until she felt herself fainting in and out. Sanity lost it. She ran outside down Keisha stairs with only a tee shirt and panties on, still holding on to one of her babies. Before they knew it the whole project could hear the sisters screaming outside and they were able to develop their own thoughts on what was going on.

Michael made his way through the crowd, "where is my baby Momma?" He ran over to Sanity and grabbed her up off of the concrete sidewalk in front of Keisha's apartment. Michael and a few of his friends came from around the corner as fast as they could to see what all the neighborhood fuss was about only to find that the best part of Sanity had been taken away from her. They helped Sanity, the kids, Keisha and her kids all get in the car so that they could go over to Big Momma house to confirm the news. When they got to Big Momma house, Sanity peeped up from the back seat and noticed the porch was surrounded with family and everyone was crying. It took four people to pull Sanity out the backseat of the car because she refused to get out and face the truth about Tim. Once they were able to get Sanity out, she looked at her cousin Tiesha and shook her head from side to side asking and begging Tiesha to tell her that none of what she was going through was true. She wanted Tiesha to tell her that Tim was in the house.

Sanity kept telling everyone he's not dead she went from person to person and told them that they just needed to wait she repeatedly said that Tim was going to walk up the street and tell everyone it was all a joke. Everyone just stared at Sanity because they knew that she was dealing with Tim's death in denial. She had blanked completely out, and the sad part was once they got her in the house the first person she ran to was Big Momma. Big Momma sat on the edge of her bed with tears flowing speechless.

"Big Momma, is it true," Sanity said.

"Is it true," all Big Momma could do was shake her head up and down slowly confirming Tim's death was true. One of Catherine's sisters yelled, "they need us to come to the hospital to identify the body." Once family members and friends of the family arrived at the hospital for Catherine to identify Tim's body Catherine walked over to Sanity and Michael and out of all the people that were there, she asked Michael to be the one to go over to Willie's boarding room and tell him about Tim's passing. Knowing that two weeks prior, Willie had approached Michael about all of the horrible rumors he had heard in the streets and it didn't go too well. Michael was with a few of his friends at the time of Willie's approach and he told Willie to his face that he didn't care about what he heard. Michael went on to deny Sanity's kids. Willie told him that he better not ever see him around Sanity or her kids again in life since Michael felt the need to show off in front of his friends in an area where the police were known to be. Catherine knew all about their disagreement and she thought it was okay for Michael to treat Sanity and their kids the way that he did. As a matter of a fact, she laughed at Sanity's pain and downfall often and people didn't mind telling Sanity every time she would talk about her kids.

Michael agreed for him to be the one to deliver the bad news to Willie about his baby boy. When the two of them arrived back to the hospital you could hear Willie's voice from the outside of the building scream, "this shit ain't true, it can't be true, my baby boy ain't dead who telling these lies?" Joe tried to stop Willie as he came through the double doors of the emergency entrance. "Where is my son? Where is the person you're calling my baby boy?" He hit the receptionist counter.

"Mr. Nova! I can't allow you to scream at me we are trying to do what's best for your family. We just don't think it would be a good idea to let you guys see his body right now because you may not be able to handle it."

"How are you going to tell me I can't see my son," Willie screamed causing the receptionist to threaten the entire family with calling security for the noise level. Sanity decided that she would be the one to call their long-distance family from Willie's side of the family.

Sanity decided she would be the one to make the call because she and Tim were so close to them. That call was devastating. After the family gathered their thoughts and feelings, everyone met back up at Big Momma and Catherine's house. All Sanity could hear was Willie cussing and fussing saying that today was not the day and he would go to jail.

"What's wrong? Why are you fussing? Now is not the time." There was so much going on and being said. Willie then told Sanity Catherine's new husband and his friends were having disrespectful side conversations about Willie being there. It pissed Sanity off because she felt it was the perfect time for Catherine to lay out some rules and demanded her new husband to respect Willie during their time of grieving. Catherine felt since she had just married her husband with the help from Sanity and everyone, she could have gotten money from to help her pay for her wedding. Catherine still had her ways of abusing everyone around her including her own mother. Before Big Momma knew it, Catherine ran through all of her sources of income including borrowing money from Big Momma and all of her life insurance policies even the ones she had for other family members.

Big Momma made sure she kept life insurance on all of Catherine and Willie's children because she was the one giving them the most care. When tax time came around every year, Willie didn't hesitate with giving Big Momma thousands of dollars to thank her for all of her help with his kid throughout the years. When it was time to lay Tim to rest, Catherine once again exhausted all of the insurance funds without paying it back so the talk went around that they didn't have enough money to bury Tim. Big Momma knew exactly how Catherine and her love for money was so she called in to another company that no one really knew about to make a claim so Tim could be buried the way he deserved to be. Catherine walked around for days embarrassed because she knew the family knew she was the one that allowed her own children's policies to cancel out. It wasn't a surprise when she told everyone that Big Momma forgot to make a payment on Tim's policy, so it was just canceled.

"The lies y'all mother tells is beyond me," Big Momma said. "I heard she out there telling someone that I didn't make a payment on my own damn grandson policy. I made sure I kept up with important stuff like that, so she needs to tell everyone the truth. She borrowed from the policy and told me that she was making payments. It wasn't until now that I found out that she was lying the whole time but yet still she loves to put the blame on everyone but herself. She really needs help."

"Big Momma we already know," Sanity said with tears rolling down her cheeks.

"If it wasn't for me having another policy on the side for y'all, my grandchild would be put in a box." Thank God Big Momma had a backup plan for the kids. After Willie got the news from Big Momma that Tim had another policy to be buried, he left as fast as he could to get away from Catherine's evil spirit.

Sanity decided to tap back into music to see if she still had it. She walked around the corner to the studio. The news had surfaced so fast around the town about Tim's passing. Everyone felt so sorry for her because they knew how much the two of them really loved and supported each other.

"What's good Sanity," Triple O said as soon as he opened the door for her to walk in. "Man, I heard the news and I don't know what to say to you." Sanity burst into tears once again. It's like the minute someone would bring up the subject she wanted to die inside. She felt like her whole life was over without Tim by her side. "Man, Sanity come in. I know you're hurt, and I don't have the riddance to say it but I'm so sorry!" They stood in the center of the floor hugging until Sanity calmed down. Triple O wiped Sanity's tears away and reminded her of how they met and how he still meant what he said when he told her and Tim that he would always be there for them no matter what.

"I know that's why I came over here," Sanity said while she was trying to get herself together wiping all of her warm tears away. After Sanity caught her breath, she told Triple O that she thought if she came over there, she could just record a song to remember Tim but the words couldn't come out. She finally told Triple O she was done with music.

"Wait no you can't do that. Your brother would not want you to give up. Come on Sanity you need to do this for him! You don't think you owe him that? He believed in you more than you believe in yourself and you can't just do my brother like that! I refuse to let you. Look I know you're hurting right now but I am too so maybe we can get past the hardest part of losing him and then revisit this music thing later. I just want you to heal first and then come back over here and let's make your brother proud."

"You're right," Sanity said as she walked towards the door to leave. She turned and thanked Triple O for always being there for her and Tim. The day of Tim's viewing, Sanity didn't have much to say to anyone that's how she chose to deal with the pain.

When they got to the door of the funeral home Catherine's sister walked ahead of everyone, she tried to reach back for Sanity's hand, but Joe pulled Sanity closer to him. Sanity also thought about how Catherine would go back and forth between the children with lies causing them to not even speak to each other. "I can't do it," Sanity yelled out trying to run away from the funeral home to keep from seeing Tim's lifeless body laying in the glossy dark grey casket. Joe pulled Sanity back to the door saying she needed to see Tim, so that the next day wouldn't be so hard on her when it was time to say her very last goodbye. "Oh God," Sanity screamed out. "Oh God no, why God why? Why how could you do me like this? I did the best I could by obeying you! I'm so sorry God, please bring him back I'm begging you God," Sanity repeated that over and over.

She cried so hard she couldn't breathe or see anything from the tears constantly rolling down her cheeks. Once Sanity made her way up to the front of the church all she could see was Tim's body sitting up higher than normal in the casket looking like he was asleep, but it wasn't a peaceful sleep. Sanity kept saying that it wasn't Tim's body that she was looking at because he did not look like himself. It took Sanity a while to finally say Tim wasn't coming back.

Weeks after laying Tim to rest, Catherine reached out to Sanity. Sounding like her whole life was over, and she really needed her there to help her get through everything. She told Catherine she would come live with her for a while because she was going through some things at home with Michael. The call came right on time for Sanity because she was back stuck in her apartment with her two sons thanks to Keisha. She agreed to help Sanity out by helping her with the kids because she knew what Tim's death did to her. Keisha kept Sanity's youngest son a lot without Sanity even asking.

Sanity sat in the house for three days waiting for Michael to return with diapers for the boys but he never did so Sanity remembered all of Big Momma's remedies in case she ever needed to use them. There were times when she had to put towels on her son and every time, he would have an accident in the towel she would throw it away until she ran out. Sanity had always been the type to go through things alone without asking any family for help because she was so afraid they would let Catherine know. Sanity made a way out of no way all on her own.

Sanity checked on her baby boy so many times a day until Keisha stopped answering. With Catherine being Sanity's mother, she thought that if her own mother did the things she did to her, then no one in the world could have been trusted. She wanted to trust her oldest sister and she knew she could trust her, but Catherine made it hard to do so. Sanity prayed every day for God to help allow her to open up and let people in so that she could get the help she needed for her children. Sanity heard a loud knock at the door as she was walking back and forth trying to put her oldest son asleep. He cried non-stop from being uncomfortable in a towel wrapped around his bottom with large safety pins on each side holding it together. The town had finally gotten a good amount of snow and she wondered who would be at her door.

"Who is it," Sanity yelled.

"It's me Michael!" Sanity ran to the door to unlock it.

Michael walked past her as fast as he could so that he could warm up, "Dang baby it's cold out there," he said to Sanity as if he was home for the past few days.

"What the hell do you mean it's cold. Yeah, it's cold out there but your kids don't have no diapers."

"I got their diapers right here," Michael handed Sanity the smallest bag of diapers that he got from the store.

"So, it took you days to bring my kids this little pack of diapers?" Sanity yelled as loud as she could. She and Catherine had spoken earlier about her moving back in with her. Sanity knew that going back around Catherine wasn't a good idea, but she felt like that was her way to escape what she was going through with her kids. After a long hour of Sanity and Michael going back and forth, Michael told Sanity that he was leaving to go to the local gym to play basketball with a few of his friends.

As soon as Michael closed the door on his way out, Sanity called the power company to have them disconnect her lights for good that time. She told them she was moving, and no one would be living there anymore. Sanity knew that she had made a very bad decision but the situation she was in wasn't any better. She felt she could start over if she left. Before the lights could be disconnected, Sanity grabbed as much of her and the kid's things as possible so that she could get her kids and leave. She walked over to her sister's place. Keisha answered the door, and it was Sanity telling her she came to get her youngest son for a while because she missed him. Keisha didn't know Sanity was leaving the projects for good because she had enough of Michael's mess. It brought back too many memories of Tim being there with her most of the time. Sanity put all of her important things along with as much clothes as she could in the bottom of the kid's stroller and walked miles in the snow to Catherine's house. When she got there Catherine didn't look happy to see her, but Big Momma was.

"Girl what are you doing out here with these babies in this kind of weather?" Big Momma asked.

"I came to stay. I thought Catherine told you I was coming."

Big Momma said, "that's crazy because she ain't mentioned a word about you and the kids coming back home." Sanity dismissed everything Big Momma was saying because she just wanted to get her babies warm and comfortable.

A few hours into Sanity relaxing on the front room couch at the house Michael called her letting her know that the power was off, and Sanity felt so good to tell him she knew.

"What you mean you know?"

"Well of course I know the lights are off because I called them to disconnect it. I mean it's no need for the lights to stay on if no one lives there anymore."

"Oh, so you're not coming back," Michael said with a chuckle in his voice thinking this was another one of their fall outs and Sanity would forgive him. Sanity laughed with him and said the joke is on you now and hung up with peace in her heart.

Living back under the same roof with Catherine was indeed hell for Sanity and her kids.

Catherine came to Sanity every week telling her what bills she needed help with. It made it hard for Sanity to save because she wasn't getting enough assistance from the government for food to support her kids, so she had decided to go back to work at the call center. She was already having it hard because she only made minimum wage and she couldn't work a lot of hours because she didn't want her kids to go hours without seeing her. Big Momma would always tell her she had her kids spoiled and it was hard for anyone to babysit them. After taking most of Sanity's income including what little the government was assisting her, Sanity was faced with depression. Her life turned in many different directions.

Chapter 33

Big Momma felt like Sanity needed to catch a breath of fresh air because she was going through so much trying to get her life together as it seemed to have been falling apart after Tim's passing. "Sanity, your friend is at the door," Big Momma said.

"Hey Big Momma." In came Sanity's best friend Jada. "Hey girl what's up," Sanity said to Jada as they walked outside to sit on the front porch.

"Sanity, see if Big Momma will keep my nephews while we go out tonight."

Sanity smiled and said, "you're right on time she just told me I need to get my butt out of this house and get some fresh air so I know she will keep them for me. She always does."

"Good," Jada said while she was dancing like she was ready to show her best friend a much-needed good time. The sun was drifting away, and Sanity started to have second thoughts about being away from her babies and what could have turned out to be an all-night thing. She had never been out all night away from her kids so that thought played over in her head while she was looking through her clothes basket to find something to wear out that night. Time flew by faster than Sanity thought she heard a horn blowing back-to-back with loud music coming from the speakers. "Sanity," Big Momma yelled down the hall, "Jada is out here blowing this horn like she's crazy. Tell her to turn that music down right now."

"Okay Big Momma,'" Sanity replied. "Are you sure you got my babies? I won't be long."

"Girl, get on out of here before I change my mind," Big Momma said laughing at Sanity pushing her towards the door so that she could leave. The next day Sanity woke up feeling so bad because she stayed out partying with Jada longer than she intended to.

"Big Momma I'm so sorry I didn't mean to stay out that late, but the time slipped right past my eye."

"Girl you okay but I'm going to let you know one thing that boy called this phone back-to-back last night and I don't appreciate his attitude when he's calling up in my house, so you better talk to him." "What boy Big Momma?"

"These kids' daddy and I told him you were gone for the night and he still kept calling, waking these boys up out of their sleep. Now you need to get that mess straight with him because he's not going to call here disturbing these kids while they are sleeping at night." Sanity called Michael immediately.

"Hello Michael, what is it," Sanity said to him. "Why are you calling here so much?"

"My mother wants to see the kids," Michael said to Sanity. "Okay that's not a problem but you can't keep calling here aggravating my grandmother she's pissed with me now."

"Okay Sanity. Just bring them over tomorrow to see my family." He hung up the phone. After not seeing where any of her paycheck was going Sanity's depression got worse. Sanity had to give as much as Catherine asked to keep a place for her and her sons. Catherine didn't mind telling people that Sanity was back at her house with her kids, but she didn't tell everyone she begged her to come back. It had only been a few months of Sanity being in the house around Catherine, but it must have been a few months too long because Catherine received a check from the insurance company for what was left over after they laid Tim to rest.

"Sanity, I found a place and I want you to get Willie's car to help move some of our things over to the new house." No matter what Catherine was putting her through, she took it because she felt like the moment she said no, then she and her kids would have ended up on the streets. Sanity drove back and forth in Willie's car scared that he would have found out she ignored what he told her.

"Okay Sanity y'all can stay here tonight. As you can see this place is small and it's only enough room in here for me and my husband. I even need to make some calls to see who Big Momma can live with because she's been here with me long enough."

Sanity dropped the last bag in her hand on the floor and said, "So Cat you mean to tell me you had me move you all day long and now you're telling me that and my kids are homeless now?"

Catherine yelled back at Sanity as if she was wrong for even thinking that she could stay there with her kids. "What the hell do you mean? Sanity, you are grown and those are your damn kids. I said my house is not that big enough and you better call around for a place for you and them kids to stay."

Sanity started laughing and walked away when she wanted to break out in tears. Sanity called every contact in her phone for a place for her and her kids. She never wanted anyone to look down on her, so she tried to make everything happen on her own. One of Sanity's Aunts called her while she was thinking as hard as she could to figure out something for not just her, but her kids and she didn't let what Catherine said go over her head because she made sure she said that Big Momma had to leave as well.

"Hey Sanity. I already heard what's going on over there. Your mother should be ashamed of herself. She goes to put y'all out and call people telling them don't let you and your kids live with them, what is her problem? I tell you one thing; I'm not going to see you and those kids on the streets like that so y'all just get a ride and you can stay here until you can get back on your feet." Sanity thought in her head that Catherine was just telling her that she was putting Big Momma out as well was just a quicker way to get rid of her so she left as soon as she could. When Sanity got to her Aunt's house, she called Willie and told him the truth that she used his car to help Catherine move only to be put out for no reason. Willie became furious with Catherine. He was mad at the world because he was so fed up with how many people she has hurt around her and it didn't seem to have bothered her one bit.

Catherine called over to Sanity Aunt's house talking about Sanity like she was a stranger almost daily. Sanity got so fed up with the many phone calls to her aunt from Catherine. Willie helped her got into a one-bedroom college student studio apartment for her and her kids and by the grace of God Willie knew the owner of the apartments. The apartments were known for loud parties from the students that lived there because the college was steps away from the campus apartments. Willie told Sanity she needed to take his car and go meet with the owner of the apartments, so she did. Sanity was all moved in and her life was back on track. She finally was approved for daycare for her kids, and everything fell right in place for them.

Sanity and Michael had a hard time trying to co-parent. Sanity imagined this great life for her kids, one that was much different from her life growing up. Michael thought things were good with him having multiple women that brought a lot of drama to Sanity's life. Threats started and the late-night disrespectful phone calls came. If he couldn't reach her on her cell phone, then he would page her with the message '187' and everyone knew that those numbers together meant murder. Sanity said to herself she wasn't going to answer any of the rude messages that came through back-to-back.

One night Sanity was in her bathroom after she had bathed the kids for bed, she heard a knock at her back door which was very weird to her because no one knew where she stayed. "Oh my God," Sanity whispered to herself quietly. All she could see was it was a man trying to get into her house. She was so scared she got on her knees to crawl to her bedroom so that she could make sure that her kids were okay. Sanity made it to the room as fast as she could, and her youngest son woke up crying. She looked at her son and placed a finger over his mouth telling him to be quiet so that the boogie man wouldn't hear them moving around in the house. Sanity called Willie over and over and got no answer. Sanity knew that whoever it was outside of her house really wanted to get inside to her and her kids. Sanity called 911 and then her mother Catherine.

"Hey what's going on Sanity," Catherine said.

"Someone is trying to get into my house, and I'm so scared I tried calling the police, but my phone is so low they keep asking me to stay calm and repeat myself. Can you hear me Cat?" Sanity said as she laid on the floor with her kids. Catherine kept saying she couldn't hear her so she hung up. Sanity was so scared she grabbed the kids and put them in her bedroom closet and covered them with clothes so that if they would cry out it would be hard for the intruder to hear them. Sanity prayed to God that he would cover them with his blood and that was the first time she had said anything to her deceased brother Tim.

"Tim, I know you're here with me," Sanity whispered. "Please protect us." The intruder tried to lift up the front room window then the noise stopped. Everything was quiet, but Sanity kept on praying to God for protection because prayer was something Sanity was very familiar with. Sanity slid her kids from the closet and just laid on top of them to protect them then she heard sirens from afar. When she heard the car door slam she ran to her door because she knew it was the policemen that time.

"Hey Sanity Nova," the police said, yelling through the door because apparently the operator was able to record Sanity's name at the beginning of her call. "Sanity, are you okay," one of the cops asked her.

"Yes, now I am! I was so scared, and I got my babies in here. What if they would have killed us," Sanity yelled, crying as hard as she could because she felt like she was near death that night. The cops took a report and said they would look into the situation then told her that they would patrol the area throughout the night. Sanity didn't know who was trying to get into her house to harm her and her children. It wasn't like she had any known enemies around town so that left her fearing for her life.

A couple of weeks later, Sanity received a call from Michael telling her to meet him at his sister's house. She refused to go so he got mad and started the name calling again. There were times he upset Sanity so bad she would walk to where he was and cause the scene he was looking for. Sanity found herself in many situations trying to prove who she really was to people that were told differently from either Catherine or Michael. The safest thing to say was that the two of them were out to get her together. Sanity always figured with Michael it was expected when people break up it could sometimes turn into a messy situation but what Catherine was doing was never heard of.

Once time went by Sanity had decided that she would meet with Michael at his sister's place so that he could see the kids. When she got there Michael told her that it was him at her window that night with a gun to end her life because he was so upset with how she left. Then he went on to say her own mother wasn't shit. Sanity mouth dropped with not a word to say because she was in disbelief her own mother would send harm to her daughter and grandchildren. Sanity was so confused until she looked at Michael asking him why her mother hates her so much.

She already asked multiple family members but did not get an answer because everyone always told her Catherine had a serious problem with telling lies and keeping drama in the entire family. She pretended to be the mother she wasn't and would start all kinds of foolishness. Sanity never confronted Catherine about what she had heard from Michael, but it wasn't the first time she kept quiet about something horrible Catherine did to her.

Sanity met a guy that was well educated, single, with no kids at the call center that she started working at. The more he tried to talk to Sanity the shyer she became towards him. No matter how hard she played to get, her team lead/supervisor at the time did not give up on trying to date her. Dating was the last thing on Sanity's mind because she didn't want to put any of her problems as a single mother on anyone else. She knew life knocked her down and she needed to stay focused to get back up and dating would have only troubled that for her.

"Hey what's up Sanity I'm Leon." A distant voice came from behind Sanity's seat where she sat daily for work.

"Hi, I don't need to give you my name because I see you already know it." Sanity said with a smirk on one side of her face. It had been a while for

Sanity to be in the company of a nice young man that wanted more from her then just sex. Sanity decided she would go on a few dates with Leon. The dates turned into long days and nights and the more time they spent together, the closer they fell for each other. The only thing bothered Sanity about Leon was his mother. She would always say little things in the background whenever he would call to check on her before he left his house for school. His mother always felt like Sanity was not good enough for her son because he was a senior in college. She called Sanity one day while Leon was at work, and she asked her why should her son be dating a woman with an already made family because Sanity had two children already and Leon didn't have any.

Leon came from a good family that had everything together they believed in higher education and marriage before children. Leon's mother would pull up to Sanity's place and blow the horn just to see the kids many days but didn't have much to say to Sanity. Sanity got fed up with the mistreatment and labeled it to Leon as disrespect. "Your mother is not right," Sanity said to Leon as they sat down to watch one of their favorite tv shows one night. "How can she just come to my house and see my kids but not have much to say to me? Like I did something to her. Just because she doesn't like the fact that I don't walk the same path that you walk." Leon put one hand on his head as if the disagreements between his mom and Sanity were starting to weigh on him. He loved Sanity but at the same time he had one of those overprotective mothers that stayed in their kids' relationships. It took Sanity a while to express her feelings about her dislikes when it came to Leon's mother. The dismissal behavior towards Sanity went on for so long it felt to Sanity that no matter who she came in contact with they would always find something wrong with her.

Catherine made her way to talk bad about her to Leon. Whenever she couldn't reach Sanity, she would call Leon's phone. She got his number from Big Momma; it was given to her in case she needed to reach Sanity while she was keeping the kids for her during her work hours or if daycare was closed. There was one day when Leon told Sanity that he wanted to take her out to the racetrack, so they got dressed and took the kids with them because the kids loved watching cars drive fast.

On their way back while the kids were taking a nap in the back seat of the car Leon said to Sanity, "baby your mom is something else ain't she?" Sanity knew right then and there that somehow some way Catherine must have said something about her to him. "Why did you say that?"

"Because she called looking for you and I told her I wasn't with you yesterday. She went on to say 'Leon you are such a great guy to Sanity, but I got one question, what in the world do you want with her'" Leon told Sanity that the question caught him off guard. He told Sanity he laughed and said "what do you mean? I'm with your daughter because I love her and her kids." He said Catherine got quiet then told him that she just asked and not to say nothing to her about it. Sanity told Leon to not answer his phone for Catherine again because if Catherine couldn't reach her then she didn't want to be reached. She also told him that her mother had been doing things like that all of her life and she didn't know why.

Sanity made sure she kept Leon away from Catherine as much as possible because she knew she was an evil woman and would do anything to see other people hurt. Catherine's jealousy started to show more and more as time went by and it showed more when Leon decided to move Sanity and her kids to a better neighborhood and give them the life that Sanity deserved. He drove multiple fancy cars and dressed like he was a millionaire to some around town. What Leon's family didn't know was that he was a schoolboy by day and a street boy by night, so yes Leon was into the fast lane lifestyle and for a little while Sanity didn't know and there were no signs of anything illegal going on. Catherine had a lot to say whenever she would see Sanity without Leon, she even thought it was funny that Michael knew people in the same area where Sanity moved to. Leon knew who Michael was and one day he came in from playing with the kids. He just looked at Sanity, smiled and shook his head.

"What," Sanity said as she started smiling.

"Hey y'all go in the bathroom so that y'all can wash y'all hands for dinner." Leon said to the kids, When the kids ran to the bathroom Leon told Sanity that while he was outside playing with the kids that Michael and some girl was only a few feet away from the kids and he looked at them several times and proceeded to walk in the house with the girl. Sanity just laughed luckily by that time she was happy with Leon and he was supportive of her and her kids without the child support checks she never received for them. Many times, Michael saw his kids and kept walking so Sanity kept on with raising her kids without the help of him. She always said that her kids would get older not younger, and they would develop their own feelings towards their father someday.

"Lord don't tell me this," Sanity said out loud as she was waking up late one night and noticed that she fell asleep on the front room couch with her front door unlocked and open while she waited for Leon to come in. She had talked to Leon off and on all day that day then all of a sudden Leon stopped responding to her texts. She got worried something bad had to have happened to him. Sanity started calling everyone she knew even the hospital.

The cops came banging on Sanity's door asking her questions about a gun that was registered to her from a drug bust they had done not far from where they lived. "Are you Sanity Nova," The cop asked her very aggressively.

"Yes, I am Sanity. Why and can you tone it down I have kids that are trying to sleep sir."

"Well, your little boyfriend won't be back home anytime soon, and I think you know exactly why Miss. Nova!"

Sanity was confused and she snapped back at him and said, "what the hell are you talking about and what damn boyfriend?" Sanity knew they were talking about Leon, but she knew the street code was not to volunteer any information. The gun belonged to Sanity. After feeling like everybody was out to get her, she went and got registered to carry a weapon for her and her children's protection and she realized she left it in one of Leon's cars. It just so happened to be one of the hottest vehicles around town that brought on a lot of attention to law enforcement. Sanity knew in her heart that Leon was doing something illegal but whatever it was he made sure he kept it away from where he rested his head which was in the home he, Sanity, and her kids shared at that time.

After a few days of no calls from Leon she started feeling like she was losing it and didn't know how to handle it. The minute she picked up her cell phone to call his mother her landline phone started ringing and she knew it had to be Leon because not many people had their landline number.

"You have a collect call from Leon." Sanity didn't know if she wanted to cry or smile.

"Hey baby," he said, sounding like he was relieved to talk to Sanity. "Leon! Leon, what is going on why the cops came here beating the door down? Leon, please tell me you didn't get into some shit you can't get out of?"

"Listen Sanity, yes I got caught up in some shit and to be honest it looks like I will have to do some time but baby please hear me out! My mother will still come by to check on y'all a few days out of the week just to make sure y'all are okay. Sanity!" Michael yelled through the phone.

"Yes, I'm here I just don't know what to say I just know that you are all we got and I don't know what to do now. I just feel so all alone already just the thought of you not being here with us tears me to pieces, how can something be so perfect and in one night it all goes bad? This is just not fair." She wiped away tears.

"Listen, I'm going to court tomorrow just try and be there if you can. I left the keys to all of the cars in the top of our closet."

"Okay I will be there," Sanity said and before she could hang up Leon told her that he loved her so much and he wouldn't be gone away from them for too long. The next day in court all Sanity heard was five years in the federal penitentiary. Sanity nearly lost her mind and her heart dropped. Before they walked Leon out in shackles, he looked over at Sanity with his eyes full of tears and said, "Sanity baby I'm so sorry for everything and I won't be mad at whatever decision you make. I just hope you make the best decision for you and my boys." Leon never said Sanity's kids weren't his. After Leon's arrest Sanity continued working and taking care of her kids but Catherine's devilish ways were still lingering around, and she would call Sanity all the time asking for rides to the store and Sanity would always make herself unavailable to Catherine. Sanity worked overtime one night and as she was getting off, she noticed she had several missed calls from Catherine. She was a little worried because she knew her kids weren't around because one of Catherine's sisters had enough and moved Big Momma in with her and her husband. So wherever Big Momma went Sanity knew it was safe for her kids to go.

Big Momma kept Sanity's youngest son most of the time because her oldest didn't mind going over to Michael's parent's house whenever she needed a babysitter for work. Jada started coming over more when she realized that Sanity was alone again and stressing about the time the judge gave Leon. Jada knew the two of them were inseparable and it was weird because their relationship was low key. It took so many people in the call center to realize that they were dating until Sanity pulled up to work in one of Leon's fancy cars while he already had one parked in the small, cluttered parking lot. All eyes were on Sanity because they were so different from each other. The one thing that stamped their love for each other was that they wanted the same things out of life like a family away from everyone, even their family. They wanted to live way out where it would take a while for someone to get to their house, a huge yard for the kids to play and make as much noise as they wanted to. Sanity started hanging out more once Leon was sent away. The few times she tried to go visit Leon, his mother would be spiteful and visit him earlier that day so by the time Sanity got there he had already used his visits for the day. That left Leon feeling like Sanity didn't want to see him because of his actions that caused him to be locked up. When Leon would call Sanity, she would miss the calls because she wasn't home. Sanity was out trying to find ways to heal all of her lifelong pain. She turned to the streets for healing.

Chapter 34

Once Leon finally was able to catch up with Sanity, he told her she really hurt him by giving up on him so soon. Sanity told Leon about all the attempts she made to see him and what happened every time she came. Leon was pissed to learn that his mother was lying to him the whole time. Sanity realized no matter how much she loved Leon his mother would always be in their way and she didn't want to deal with that. Sanity told Leon to hang up and call back because the automatic system said there were only thirty seconds to talk and she needed to have a quick heart to heart with him. When Leon called back, she told him she loved him and him not being there was really hard for her. She also told him that it was hard enough so she didn't know if she could do it with his mother in the way of them fully loving each other.

"Sanity I completely understand but I have tried to talk to her a million times, and you know how she is."

"I know that's why I will be honest and tell you that

I will try my best to wait on you but if it gets too hard, I may have to pull myself away from this and see what happens when you get out." They came to an agreement that it would go the way that Sanity wanted it to.

After hanging out around a few of the wrong people in the streets and learning the trending recipe for curing any pain, Sanity was way off track. Sanity made sure that her kids were well taken care of before

late-night missions For five months of Sanity's
nightlife adventures she attempted a popular drug and
decided it wasn't for her. It would numb the pain
until the high went down and once the high was gone
the pain came back but stronger. Catherine heard that
Sanity was in the streets and that was all she needed
to try and wheel Sanity back in under her devilish
spell. Catherine started catching rides to the areas
where she heard Sanity would be. Catherine finally
caught up with Sanity to tell her that she was going
through so much and had no one to turn to. She told
Sanity her husband had cheated on her and was good
for nothing around the house. Sanity was so surprised
to hear that because Catherine's husband was very
quiet and kind of stayed to himself.

After hearing so many horrible things
Catherine was going through Sanity actually felt bad
for her only because Sanity knew that pain as well. A
little time went by and Catherine needed help paying
her power bill and Sanity had some extra money
saved up from what Leon left her. Sanity wanted to
do what was right, so she paid Catherine's power bill
because she knew what it felt like to be in the dark.
Sanity also remembered when Willie and Catherine
first separated, they went through pure hell their
power was off for five months straight they were
fortunate enough to run a big orange drop cord from
their back door to the neighbors that live behind their
house front door. They used to call that borrowing
power back in the good old days.

There were many days Big Momma would
say if only her husband were alive, she would not

have gone through that type of struggle. Sanity's Grandfather had died early on in their lives from congestive heart failure, but Big Momma still hung in there through it all. After Sanity paid Catherine's power bill, Catherine started calling more and more needing money every time. She never asked about her grandchildren; it was always about what she needed and how bad things were for her. The more Sanity gave the more Catherine asked and if she didn't, she would be called every name under the sun.

"Let's go out tonight," one of Sanity's friends said that she had met during her nightlife.

"Alright let's do that. Where the hell are we going? You know I can't stay out all night because Big Momma got my son and my other son is at his grandparents house for tonight." Sanity and a group of friends went out later that night and had the best time of their lives. That night ended horribly for her because they stayed in the club all night partying. Once they left, they all stayed over Jada's house because they were too high and drunk to even function. She called Big Momma to apologize but Big Momma wasn't trying to hear that she yelled and told Sanity she really needed to get her shit together.

When Big Momma hung up on her she cried for the longest asking God to forgive her. Sanity called Big Momma back as the day was fading away. "Sanity! Don't come and get the baby right now because he's enjoyed himself. I will call you when he starts all that crying mess," she laughed and hung up. That was what Sanity needed to hear because she had made calls to several shelters in Atlanta looking for placement. She had even had a job lined up near the shelter and luckily there was a daycare center for residents that stayed at the shelter with kids. Sanity had made up her mind that she wanted to leave everything behind and relocate to a place she and Tim disagree on living together. She knew things would be really rough starting over, but she also knew things were worse where she was. Sanity packed up all of her and the children's clothes and anything that she could fit in two big suitcases. She let Catherine know that she was leaving to start over. No matter what Catherine did to her she would always forgive her and try to start over, so she wanted to see Catherine face to face before her bus left. Sanity called Catherine and told her after she picked her kids up that she needed to talk to her because it may be a while before she saw them again. She told her she needed to go far away. Catherine was confused she didn't know what Sanity was trying to tell her. They agreed to meet in the projects because she was going to a card game. While Sanity listened to gospel music and packed her things, she received a call from one of her long-distance cousins that moved away years ago. As soon as Catherine hung up she had told everyone at the card table Sanity was leaving town.

"Hey Sanity, it's me Tina! I'm the girl that use to hang with your cousin Tiesha on your mother's side. I got your number from my sister because she's at the card game with your mother."

"Oh, hey what's up? I know who you are. I remember you. It's good hearing from you, what you got going on?"

"Oh nothing! I was calling because I heard you was moving and you're leaving soon?"

"Well damn how do you know that?" Sanity said. "Your mom must have said something at the card
game and I was talking to my sister. I told my sister shit you can come up here to Highpoint Nc with me because I ain't got no man." Tina laughed. Sanity was very hesitant, but Sanity knew that she was getting out one way or another. She told her that she needed to think about it. By the time she got ready to leave she told her to give her a few minutes to call her back with an answer.

"Okay Tina, but I promise you will love it here. I can show you around, you should really come here." Sanity called Tina back and told her she would try it out. In her mind, she knew she needed to go away from Catherine and needed to not ever look back because Catherine made her life a living hell. Sanity only decided to tell Catherine because she needed to face her pain before she started over.

"Sanity! Now what was you saying on the phone? You said you leave? Child you will not make it trying to go live in some big ass city by yourself with them little kids tuh! You'll be back!" Sanity was so embarrassed until she felt herself shaking ready to break but she held it together and told Catherine.

"No, I won't!" Catherine thought that the joke was on Sanity, but the joke was really on her. Catherine jumped up from the table and asked Sanity to walk outside with her once they got outside, she gave Sanity a balled up twenty-dollar bill and told her to call her sometime. Sanity refused the money over and over but since Catherine insisted, she took the money and the fake hug that Catherine gave her.

Sanity left town leaving her entire family and a very nice apartment full of furniture and food. She decided once she walked away, she was walking away with nothing. A few months in the new city Sanity got a call from Catherine asking for money again this time she told her it was for some important medicine that she needed. Sanity refused to send it then once she started feeling bad, she sent it. Catherine had her way with getting what she wanted out of anyone. Catherine's verbal abuse got so bad towards Sanity until she couldn't take it anymore, so she blocked her number from her phone. Two years passed and Sanity found herself homeless again because the girl that she moved in with took her and her kids through hell. Sanity had to chump some stuff up until she could get herself together. Sanity applied for welfare and food stamps. The same week she relocated, Sanity noticed a change in Tina's kid's behavior towards her kids because Sanity's kids weren't comfortable around people that they didn't know. Sanity spent a lot of time teaching her sons how to respect everyone no matter who they were. Tina's kids started calling them names and mistreating them the minute Sanity turned her back away. One of her children even attempted to pour bleach in one of Sanity's son's cups. Sanity had enough of it and told Tina the things her kids were doing. Tina refused to handle it the way that a mother should have.

Sanity took her kids with her everywhere she went on the local city bus to look for jobs. Many places she went to the employers talked bad about her, but she did what she needed to do and if that meant job hunting with her kids because she didn't have a babysitter then that's what she did. Sanity became so overprotective of her kids that she took them everywhere she went she even snuck them on to her new job she had just started at. It was one of the hospitals as a housekeeper. Sanity made $7.25 an hour cleaning patient's rooms for a living. This was all she had to support her and two children. It made things so much harder for Sanity. She was already sleeping on a couch with her two kids in a two-bedroom apartment with a family of four that didn't belong to her, so she was very uncomfortable every single day. Tina did not care if she was comfortable or not and although Sanity was going through all of that she still didn't think about going back to her hometown.

One day while Sanity was writing out her feelings, she received a call from an unknown number. It was one of her neighbors from back at home where she left and was telling her that Catherine came to her door and wanted to know if she knew who owned the house that Sanity lived in because she needed to get into the house. The neighbor said she told Catherine hold on she would get the number but instead she called her right away.

"Wow! So did she say what she needed to get into my house for?" Sanity asked her neighbor.

"No, she just said that you said she could get your furniture. Yeah, I think that's just what she said." Sanity was so fed up with Catherine she told her neighbor to let her get whatever was in there. That was how done Sanity was with everything, and she knew that she didn't plan on returning.

"Okay Sanity but are you okay because baby you don't sound like you are?" Sanity didn't want to lie so she told her, no she wasn't okay.

"But I will be. I'm just going to keep on pushing because I know God got me," she said with confidence. Sanity had been working at the hospital for a while in the same department, but things were looking a little better for her because she finally got the kids into a daycare that ran 24/7 and it was perfect for Sanity because she didn't mind working extra hours for more money. Welfare took all benefits away from her because she was working.

Sanity finally met a guy she called her friend at the time. He showed her around the city a few days out the week. He would always see her standing at the bus stop waiting to go home. When his car broke down and he ended up on the same bus as Sanity. He wasted no time telling her that he saw her a lot at that same stop, and it was him blowing the horn. Sanity wasn't trying to hear anything the guy had to say. He had a sense of humor, but she still didn't pay that much attention. She met a really nice young lady that worked at the hospital with her. They did everything together to even testing positive for pregnancy together. Sanity knew her body and she knew it was a strong possibility after her and the guy she met decided they would hang out a lot. Sanity decided to go to the emergency room to get the test done over just to make sure that the results were real.

"Well Sanity congratulations! You are definitely pregnant."

Sanity looked at her friend and said, "how could this happen I mean how could this happen right now. I'm already going through a lot trying to raise my other two sons. There's no way I could be a mom again. Things are just so hard for me right now. I have nothing to offer another kid right now so what am I going to do?"

Her friend looked at her and smiled, "Sanity I promise we will get through this together!" Sanity got to work the next day and called her guy friend from the hospital wall phone with her friend standing right at her side as she promised she would.

"Hey, we need to talk," Sanity said as soon as he answered the phone. He automatically assumed something was wrong.

"What's up?"

"Well, I'm pregnant," Sanity said.

His response was, "so what are you going to do." "What do you mean what am I going to do? I mean I'm pregnant and that's what it is!" He told Sanity that he wasn't ready for a child and he knew that she wasn't ready for another child. Sanity hung up because she knew that he didn't want to man up. Sanity stopped seeing him and decided she wasn't going to give him what he wanted. She would have her child and do the best that she could.

She started applying for better jobs making more money but every time she got past the interview, they would ask her to bring in a copy of her high school diploma. Sanity knew that She couldn't because she had dropped out of school in the eleventh grade when she got pregnant with her oldest son and she never went back. That was the one thing that kept Sanity in poverty. As long as she didn't have a piece of paper that said she graduated from high school her life would continue to go through hell because she wouldn't be able to work anywhere that would pay her enough to support three children on her own.

Sanity started showing as she was carrying her now third child, but Sanity was looking bigger than normal, so she decided to go to the doctor because she was feeling some weird pain. Sanity learned that day that she was carrying twins inside of her belly. Sanity told the doctor to take another look because she did not believe it. Sanity couldn't believe what the doctor was telling her. She thought to herself how in the hell could she have taken care of four children by herself with no place to call home. She jumped up to put her clothes on so that she could hurry to call her new friend to let her know what the doctor just told her. She needed someone to talk to and knew she couldn't call anyone back home.

As time went by and Sanity got bigger, she called Catherine herself just to let her know that she was having another baby and all Catherine said was "oh okay" but that's the reaction Sanity expected. Sanity situation looked like it wasn't getting any better for her, it seemed like the harder she worked the more money she had to spend just to provide food and childcare for her children. Sanity started getting really stressed because she let Catherine back into her life by unblocking her from her phone hoping and praying that Catherine would change her ways and they could really develop a bond. Catherine only stressed Sanity out even more as she continued to ask her for money and if Sanity couldn't give it to her, she would call her all types of names and talk bad about her to anyone that she could. She would also go around town spreading rumors saying Sanity was on drugs and didn't take care of her kids just to make Sanity look bad. Sanity knew long before then that Catherine would have done anything to harm her character. Every time something got back to Sanity, she found out that Catherine was the one spreading the nasty rumors about all of her children.

Sanity built up even more anger inside. She couldn't even go around people without having an attitude. Sanity became very aggressive and even more protective of her kids. Sanity didn't trust anyone with her kids because she always felt that if her own mother would take her through what she went through then anybody in the world would do it. She just became so overwhelmed with her life.

It was 3:00 a.m. when Sanity decided she really needed to call Catherine one morning because she had been up for hours crying to tell her how she hurt her all of her life. Catherine answered the phone sounding really sleepy, but Sanity felt like if she didn't tell her then it would be never.

"Hey Cat, I know you're asleep, but we need to talk. I have been crying all day and I just need to tell you how I feel." Catherine told Sanity that she was tired and would call her back the next day. Sanity waited on Catherine's call the next day because she stayed up all night crying asking God why. Catherine never called so Sanity called her back. This time Catherine was at a card game so Sanity needed to talk so bad she didn't care that time either so she asked Cat to step outside of where she was so that they could have a serious talk. That time Catherine yelled at her and told her she did not have time to talk to her about old shit. Before Sanity hung up, she told Catherine to have a good day because as bad as Sanity wanted to curse Catherine out, she never did.

At Sanity's doctor appointment the doctor discovered that one of her twin babies didn't have a heartbeat and they needed to monitor her. Sanity was crushed because by that time her bond was strong with her babies that she was carrying and she knew that God gave her more to love. She walked around a lot because she was sleeping on either the couch or the floor every night and she heard that she could get a blood clot while she was pregnant. Sanity caught the city bus with her two children and big belly just about every single day. Sanity's pregnancy was hard because she was so big, but she was very healthy besides the stress. The doctor ended up telling Sanity that one of her babies heartbeat had for sure completely stopped and it would be hard for them to remove the baby because the other twin was on top. Sanity cried days and nights trying to figure out if she was better off dead. That's when the thought came to Sanity's head to just end her life. She also thought that if she ended her life, she would get to be with Tim. Sanity felt like she was all prayed out and her life was only falling apart. She panicked and got the kids dressed so they could catch the city bus to the emergency room after the news she had gotten about her twins. Every feeling in her body freaked her out but she was okay that night. The next day Sanity caught the bus to the daycare to drop the kids off so that she could go back to get some rest. While she was asleep, her phone rang, and the number looked really familiar, so she answered.

"Hello," the man said.

"Hi who is this," Sanity asked.

"Wow I can't believe your number is still the same," Leon said in a complete shock. Sanity started crying out loud holding her belly trying to figure out a way to tell him that she was having another child.

"Leon oh my God are you for real." They both laughed. They caught up on some old memories and times then Leon asked Sanity if she was willing to come and see him if he sent for her or came and got her. Sanity told Leon she would, but she needed to tell him something. He started laughing and said, "I already know you're pregnant with twins and there's nothing I can do about that, but I still want and need to see you. So can you do that for me?"

Sanity told Leon yes, she thought it would be better if he sent for her because it gave her more time to think on a long bus ride. As soon as Sanity got off the bus in her old hometown there Leon was standing there smiling with red eyes as if he was crying. They hugged each other so tight for so long. Leon grabbed Sanity's bags and stared at her with the biggest smile on his face. In that moment it was like they fell in love with each other all over again. While they were in the car revisiting their past, Sanity kept trying to apologize to Leon for not waiting on him but he kept stopping her. Sanity told Leon her life was in shambles and he needed a woman that came with less baggage because she came with a lot. She told him that she tried to wait but the longer she waited the more shit she went through. She also told him it was things she went through before she even met him. Leon agreed and told Sanity he understood. He said so much time had gone by and he didn't blame her because he knew what she was dealing with when it came to Catherine anyway. He also knew that things were better for Sanity during their relationship because he was there with her. He told Sanity he knew she would have gotten tired and up and moved away someday and he wished her the best.

When he got out, he was facing more charges and he had to be home by a certain time so it would have made things much more complicated with them because she was so far away, so they agreed to go their separate ways. A few weeks later the same weird feeling came back in Sanity's body only this time it was worse her whole leg went numb and she couldn't walk. Sanity called 911 after the operator heard the children in the background, they told her that she needed to see if someone could keep them when the medic arrived Sanity started screaming at the operator because she was so scared and had never felt that feeling before. Sanity was forced to make a call to her unborn child's father as soon as she told him what was going on, he rushes over to her place. Once her child's father arrived, he rushed her and the kids to the hospital because it was hard for her to walk because her leg was losing feeling. The closer they got to the emergency room.

When they arrived, the nurse knew something bad was going on because her face was also abnormally swollen.

"Hurry hurry!" One tall Caucasian doctor ran in the room. The assistant had a hard time drawing blood from Sanity. It took her five tries before she was successful with getting the amount of blood she needed. She asked Sanity if she made sure that she was staying hydrated throughout her pregnancy as she was doing her blood work. After rushing Sanity to the maternity ward, all Sanity could hear was a room full of doctors standing around her saying that they needed to remove her unborn child away from her immediately and a woman doctor yelling saying that they needed to give her a few rounds of steroids to pump the baby's lungs because it was way too soon to give birth. Sanity's whole body felt like it was shutting down, she started sweating uncontrollably. It felt like her life was ending, her body was in pain from head to toe and it seemed like the doctors didn't know how to help her. That's when Sanity heard one of the doctors say something that she never thought she would have. He said Sanity things are not looking good for you because your blood pressure is sitting in the stroke zone and your body is not responding to any of the medications that we are giving you. The doctors felt as if they did everything that they could to get Sanity stable and we're all out of options.

They told the father of the child to try to contact Sanity's next to kin so they could tell them what was going on with her. Sanity prayed as hard as she could, in her mind she told God that if he didn't do anything else for her to please spare her life so that she could continue to raise her two kids that she already had. Sanity felt like her life was ending by the seconds until she heard Catherine on speaker phone while the doctor explained to her what was going on. She said, "well I'm all the way in another city and there's nothing that I can do right now. I told Sanity having these babies was no joke. Well call me when it's over." Sanity wanted to die but she knew she had so much to live for, so she never stopped praying. She knew exactly how powerful God was and she kept the faith. Sanity's body went through so much unbearable pain and not a word came out of her mouth because she was unable to talk from being so swollen. Sanity was in labor for four days straight with contractions and all she could do was cry. Her friend TeTe that she met while working at the hospital came to see her while she was facing one of the worst days of her life. TeTe was humble and sweet and no matter what life brought her way she would weather the storm with a big smile on her face. She had been there with Sanity through it all as promised and no matter what she was going through in her personal life or pregnancy, she never left Sanity's side. She rushed to the maternity ward once she got off work and heard Sanity was in labor. She begged Sanity and the kids to come and live with her before she got her own apartment, but Sanity didn't want to put her situation off on anyone else. Four days after hard labor and a whole lot of prayer Sanity had given birth to her third underweight but healthy baby boy.

Sanity woke up not knowing where she was or in fact who she was everything the doctors said was a blur. She had become confused, so they gave her more medication. The next day Sanity woke up there was a light skinned woman sitting at the foot of her hospital bed holding her hand with one of Sanity's long-distance cousins. She heard from the young lady Tina that Sanity moved in with when she first relocated to the city. She was one of Sanity's cousins that knew the struggle well. Her background was just as worse as Sanity's. Sanity and her siblings didn't grow up around that side of her mother's family because Catherine never took them around. The doctor asked her to leave the room while she talked to Sanity in private.

"Sanity sweetheart do you know where you are?"

"No Sanity said and where is my baby?"

"He's fine. He's in the NICU but I have to say Sanity he's doing so great but you're not. You're on the sick maternity ward with the women who had complications during delivery." The doctor told Sanity that it took days to figure out what was wrong with her. She said, "Sanity you got one of the worst cases we have seen in a while of preeclampsia and your case is severe. We will still need to monitor you for some days before we can release you. Do you feel like your body is full of fluids?" The doctor asked.

"Yes, my legs feel heavy, and I can't move them."

"Well, your weight is now 398 pounds and I know it could be very uncomfortable, but I gave you some medication in your IV with hopes that we can at least get the fluid down. Sanity your blood pressure is extremely high, and we are doing everything we can to get you to feeling better." Sanity started crying again causing the vital machine to beep nonstop causing Sanity to shake. "Sanity...Sanity, honey I need you to calm down because you're only getting yourself sicker and we don't want that, your kids really need you."

Even though Sanity felt like she was slowly slipping away she looked at the doctor and yelled back at her and said, "No I really need them." The doctor gave Sanity some strong medication so that she could relax as she watched Sanity drifted off to sleep. A week and a half later Sanity was finally ready to meet her new baby boy. The nurse rolled Sanity to the NICU to see him, and Sanity was speechless because it was the first time that she was able to hold her son in her arms since she gave birth to him. She started feeling lightheaded after about an hour of bonding with her son, so she asked the nurse to take her back to her room. Once she got to the room she asked if she could take a shower because that would have been her first time getting in the shower since she gave birth, the doctor ordered her to have only bed baths while she continued to try and get better. As soon as the nurse left the room Sanity got in the shower and Sanity's body took no time going into a shock from the hot steam. Sanity felt herself falling to the floor and tried to yell for help as loud as she could, but no one could hear her from the bathroom door being closed. A few minutes later her nurse rushed to her room because Sanity was able to pull the alarm for help before she hit the floor.

When she got in the bathroom, she called Sanity's name, but she wasn't responding. Her eyes were rolling around in her head she whispered in a very low voice "please help me I don't feel good." The nurse called for help and they assisted Sanity back to her bed after doing so they checked her vitals. They moved Sanity closer to the nurse's station so that they could keep an eye on her and wouldn't waste any time getting to her if they needed to.

Sanity was discharged from the hospital two weeks after she had her son, but she was unable to take him home with her because he was so underweight. They could not keep his temperature up to where it needed to be to be discharged. The doctors called Sanity every other day to come and get her son but every time she got there, they would tell her that he didn't pass the breathing test and it would be the next day before he could be released. That stressed her out so bad she cried all day and night. She started to worry about her health a lot at every checkup she would cry and asked the doctor if she would make it to see her kids grow up. Sanity became very nervous about everything especially when her sons would play with toys that caused a lot of noise. It would cause her to have palpitations until it felt like her heart was jumping out of her chest and throughout all of that she didn't hear a word back from Catherine. She never called Sanity to check on her even after the horrible phone call she got the day Sanity was rushed to the hospital.

Sanity stressed about that a lot because in her head Sanity knew that no matter what she did her mother didn't care if she lived or died as long as she gave her everything she wanted, Sanity worked hard for on her own. The day came and it was time for Sanity to pick up her baby boy from the hospital. Sanity's friend TeTe couldn't have been happier. She was the one that refused to let Sanity ride the bus after all she was going through with her health and mental. Once Sanity got the baby home later that day the nurse came by to pay a visit to Sanity just to check and see how she was doing and to check her vitals. Sanity had to have special treatment for her health condition because it was hard for her to maintain going out in public.

"Sanity you're not getting any better dear. What are you doing to relax? The nurse said, after you get the kids together for bed" Sanity looked at her and told her she wanted to get better but didn't know how. That's when the nurse told Sanity that they needed to put her on four different blood pressure medications along with some anxiety medication. She knew once she started her medications her health would get back to normal and she would be able to take care of her children without worrying about if she was going to live or die.

Months passed and she was still battling her health issues. Catherine finally called Sanity and asked her what she was doing but not how she was doing. Sanity went ahead and told Catherine she wasn't doing well and was on so many different medications and Catherine told Sanity something that was so familiar, she told her that having babies wasn't a joke. She felt herself getting upset so she told Catherine that she would call her back and before Sanity hung up Catherine asked her for money. Sanity told her as nice as she could that she wasn't working because she was sick and had just given birth to a child but that went right over Catherine's head. She really didn't care; she just wanted money. Sanity wasn't getting any better, but she knew she needed to work.

She started working at a nursing home as a nursing assistant. She always had a helping heart since she was fifteen years old. The company Catherine attempted to work at for about a month was illegal, so Catherine fit right in with them. The day Sanity went there for Catherine to cover her shift, she sent her 15-year-old daughter at the time in a taxi and told her the owner would tell her what she needed to do once she got there. When Sanity got there the owner of the house told her to come and sign a sheet that had lots of names on it, but when Sanity went to write her name the lady got an attitude with her and told her that she needed to put another name down because if the state came in she would get in trouble for having an minor working. Sanity worked eight hours with no pay because when payday came Catherine took the money for herself and never told Sanity thank you for going to work for her. Sanity was able to bond with the clients and grew to love that kind of work.

Working at the nursing home and being underpaid was so hard for Sanity physically and mentally but again she was forced to do what she needed to. She would talk to her oldest Sister Keisha off and on throughout her time in the big city. Keisha knew Sanity started working at another job and she was very happy for her, but Sanity still didn't know how to talk to her about what she was going through with her health. Keisha just didn't seem to have the words to say but she would always tell Sanity to be careful. Keisha must have mentioned it to Catherine. Catherine started calling Sanity every other day talking about everyone in their family, even her sisters and brother since Joe had heard how bad Catherine talked about him to his girlfriend. He stopped speaking to Catherine completely and no matter what no one said to him he refused to see her face. It was told that Catherine said that she felt that the wrong son died which confused everyone. Once again Sanity fell back into her stupid ways and started helping Catherine again. This time Catherine put her love for money on her health. Every time she called it was about her payments for her doctor visits or some new medication, she needed to be able to walk because her blood pressure was also out of whack.

After Sanity got so many texts from her about her health, she started to believe that Catherine was sicker than she thought. After about a year of working at the nursing home, Sanity began to get even more sick. Her heart was beating so fast at work she started sweating. She sat down to check her own heart rate from the nurse's station. When she saw that she had been sitting down for an hour and her resting heart rate was at 170 bpm, she knew something was wrong. She decided to go to the emergency room after her manager told her that she couldn't stay at work under those conditions. They told her that her heart results didn't look normal. Sanity had a follow up appointment the next day with her primary doctor and they told her she needed to wear a heart monitor.

Sanity was losing all of her hope in getting better. She was starting to think maybe she was better off dead that way she wouldn't feel any pain from anywhere or anybody. When she wore her heart monitor it caused her to be ashamed. She did what the doctors asked her to do. After putting all of her children to bed and turning on gospel music to pray her way through the sound of the bullets flying over her apartment, she heard her heart monitor beeping and she tried pressing through the noise. She snatched her monitor off and started yelling and crying out to God asking him to heal her body and protect her children. Her next step was to the refrigerator to grab a bottle of wine that someone told her would relax her mind and before she knew it she drank the whole bottle and wanted more. The more she drank the more she forgot about her problems. After drinking so much she woke up late the next day for work. Sanity caught the bus to the daycare to drop the kids off then she did a walk-in at her doctor office to let them know that she was going to trust in God and no longer wanted to wear the monitor. The front desk receptionist told her to calm down and the doctor would come out and talk to her.

"Sanity I get that this is a lot for you, but we need to figure this out together." Sanity held her head down twisting her fingers like a helpless little girl because she was so tired. After the doctors tried Sanity on a new set of medications, she started feeling like herself again. She stopped talking to Catherine and her life was changing by the days. Sanity still had to deal with the gunshots and loud music every night, but she would try and tune it out with gospel music. She and her children spent more time in church so she could get closer with God. She was going through a lot, but she still didn't know what her purpose was in life and she wanted to know that more than anything in the world.

Years passed and Sanity received a call from one of her family members saying Catherine was going through hell. When she asked what kind of hell, she was told that Catherine was losing everything, her house and her mind.

"Hey Cat, how are you this is my new number and I wanted to just check in on you."

Catherine started laughing, "Oh God hey Sanity. How are the kids doing?"

"Fine. They are at daycare right now." Sanity stretched her eyes wider because that was the first time Catherine asked her how her sons were doing. Going to church taught her a lot, it taught her how to love the ones that hurt her because they would have to answer to God someday. She decided to keep in touch with Catherine despite what Catherine had put her through because she knew that someday Catherine would see her wrong and would apologize to her for all of the pain that she caused in her life. Sanity also learned that no matter how bad you lie or how much you try to hide the wrong you do to people the truth will come out if you just wait on the Lord.

After contacting Catherine, she started feeling ill again but this time she figured it was from the stress of where she was living because it seemed like every week someone got killed in her neighborhood. Most of the time it was innocent bystanders, some were even kids. She really feared her and her kid's life and money were starting to run low because she was unable to go to work on the days she was sick. The homeless program she went through to get her apartment kept in touch with her so they sent her to a few food pantries so she could get food for them. Her doctor ended up writing a letter to the CEO of the projects where she lived to have her relocated to one of their sister complexes with less violence especially after she saved up to purchase her first car and weeks later it was stolen right from out front of her apartment overnight. It took them two weeks to call her with an offer to be moved to a better environment. Sanity was so excited to get the good news that she was moving her kids to a better place.

She called TeTe as soon as she got the call, and she was over at her house in twenty minutes.

"Girl I told you God got you," TeTe said. Sanity and TeTe were so close people thought they were real sisters. Sanity's kids called TeTe auntie and TeTe kids called Sanity auntie. Since Sanity got the great news about her moving, she decided that it was time and she really needed to go back to school to get her high school diploma, but she also wanted to go back into the customer service world because she had a lot of fun there. She moved into her new place and the kids were so happy she said to herself okay God I've been tricked all of the other times into believing that things were changing for me! God, I know that this is the moment where things are really going to change for me and my babies because you said it in your word.

Being in her new place for a week was the best feeling she had in a while even though it was still public housing. It was so much different from where she moved. There was no loud music, fighting, gunshots, children cursing or knocking on her door. One thing was missing for Sanity and that was a good paying job so that she could support her kids. Since her rent was not even a hundred dollars, Sanity decided to step out on faith to continue her education, but she needed to know where to start.

Sanity got up early one morning, got her kids dressed and proceeded to walk through a very long dark path. The path had torn up clothes, soda cans, and beer bottles but she noticed in the soda cans it had burnt holes poked in them, so she knew what that look like because she grew up around that type of behavior from different family members, so she knew that they use cans to smoke crack cocaine that's when Sanity grabbed her head and said, oh God not again! What in the hell have I gotten myself into this time? but it was the only way she could make it to the bus stop to catch a city bus, so she kept on walking until she came face to face with a drunk lady telling her to be careful because women were known for getting rapped in that path. She told the lady thank you and pulled all of her kids close to her. After she got off the bus, she had to walk her children four miles to the daycare but she didn't mind because she was so comfortable in her new apartment and all she could do was thank God for bringing her that far. Once she got the kids settled in at the daycare there was no way around her walking back through the path to get back to her apartment, so she walked back through the path but this time she didn't go back to her apartment. She went to the rent office to see what kind of information they had for becoming self-sufficient.

"Well, hi Mrs. Nova," the property manager said to Sanity as she walked in with a big smile on her face.

"Hi! Sanity said as she reached out to shake the woman's hand.

"No honey I need to give you a hug," the woman said, pulling Sanity close to her. "Have a seat Sanity and let's chat because girl we forgot you live out here you just stay to yourself huh?"

"Yes, ma'am I don't even want to get to know anyone that lives out here. I just want to better myself," Sanity said to the woman.

"Oh my," the woman said as she shook her head from side to side. She looked at Sanity and told her that she was the first young lady that came to her and asked for help. She went on to say that girls had been living there for over five years with nothing going on. The program was a five-year program and the money you used to pay your rent went into an account to assist you with buying a house once you leave the program. Sanity wanted nothing more than to use that opportunity to give her children a better life. The property manager gave her paperwork to fill out. The paperwork was to help her get her high school diploma. Sanity also checked out a customer service specialist program. Once the woman got the completed paperwork back from Sanity, she looked over it twice then she smiled and got up from behind her desk to give Sanity another big hug. She told Sanity that she knew she would do well with the program because she was so ambitious and determined to do better and Sanity couldn't agree more.

Sanity started school without having to pay a dime because the program paid everything including extra funding for the kids to continue going to daycare. When she asked her school instructor about her book fees, she told her that her package was completely taken care of by her program. manager. After scary mornings and long nights, Sanity became very frustrated with school and work, but she knew she came too far to turn back. She had to get her children dressed at 4:00a.m every morning Monday through Friday to get them to before school care, so she could catch the bus to work eight hours and then school giving her only two hours in between both. She worked and went straight to school sometimes with nothing to eat all that day either because she was trying to make sure her kids had enough to eat, or she just lost her appetite from stress. Time flew by before Sanity knew it and it was time for her to graduate. She reached out to Catherine months prior to her graduation day and sent her invitations so that her and a few other family members could finally get to see her march across the stage. She knew Big Momma would have been there and she had lost contact with Willie because she was too busy trying to hide what she was going through.

Sanity wouldn't talk to anyone that tried to make her move back to the hell hole she left so she distanced herself. On graduation day, of course no one showed up. She didn't even see her kids in the audience, but by the time she heard her name to march she looked to her right and there were her three sons smiling and pointing at her because her friend made sure she brought them. She broke down crying holding her stomach because her heart was so full of joy just to look out at the smile on her children's face meant everything to her. She dismissed the fact that Catherine or no one else was there. This wasn't a surprise to Sanity at all because she was used to it. She only came around when it benefited her and seeing Sanity graduate wasn't a benefit to her at all.

Shortly after graduation Sanity applied for a job at a local popular call center in the city. She was very nervous because in order to get the position you had to pass a test and looked to Sanity like more people were failing the test than passing it and that tore Sanity's nerves up. When it was time for her to take the test, she met a very nice lady that was waiting who was also nervous. The lady and Sanity clicked just like her and TeTe did when they first met. Sanity and the lady took the test, and both passed it with flying colors. They both were so happy that they passed so they exchanged numbers and went their separate ways.

Sanity called the lady Tammie's phone because they kept in contact over the time. The two of them became really close friends and their kids played together almost every day. It didn't take Tammie long to find out everything that Sanity was going through. She noticed that Sanity was sending money to someone more often than she should have been being as though she was struggling so badly herself as a single mother of three young children. Sanity also learned that Tammie was struggling with multiple kids herself, so the two of them started struggling together. After taking Sanity to wire money so many times Tammie confronted Sanity about what she was doing. All she would say was, "I know but I'm just helping my mother out because she is going through a lot." Tammie left the conversation alone and didn't mention it again because no matter what she said Sanity would still do it.

Tammie had been working with the tax company for over fifteen years and that was a good thing for Sanity because she would just let her file her taxes for her each year. When her friend noticed that she was sending a lump sum of money more around that time of year she started asking her more questions. Catherine fell hard and really needed help with getting her own taxes filled so she asked Tammie if she would help her with getting hers done. It was a long process with Catherine's paperwork because she had been claiming kids that didn't belong to her for so many years. Catherine was facing debt with the IRS. She told Sanity that was all she needed to get where she needed to be financially. Sanity figured if Tammie could assist her that would be great because she had complained for years about the person that did her taxes screwed them over each year and over charged her for filing her taxes. Since Tammie and Sanity were so close, she would do anyone's taxes that Sanity brought to her. She wouldn't even charge them most of the time.

Catherine needed Tammie's phone number so that she could keep in touch with her throughout the filing process so Sanity gave it to her because she would text her asking her questions about her refund and get mad when she couldn't respond. Catherine had this very bad evil habit where she would send you messages telling you what God would do to you if you didn't obey her as the mother. Sanity was so aggravated with the calls and messages she finally gave in and gave Catherine the number so that her life would be a little bit easier with the disrespect from her. Before you knew it Sanity and Tammie were years into working their new job at the call center and they loved it so much they rode together every day. Tammie had to stop Sanity from catching the city bus. She begged Sanity every day to allow her to take her back and forth to work especially when she saw how hard it was for her to get her children together. She told Sanity she didn't know how she held it together so perfectly because in her eyes it looked perfect, but Sanity just had to learn how to make the struggle look good for her sons. Sanity noticed Catherine stopped calling and believe it or not she was so relieved. The minute Sanity would think everything was all good Catherine would start her mess again but this time she would accuse Sanity of talking about her or she would tell her God was going to punish her for lying. No matter how respectful Sanity was to Catherine, she still would send her even more disrespectful text messages. Sanity started to have an attitude daily. She was angry, waking up and going to sleep. Even her kids noticed a change in her attitude, so they started asking her if she was okay. Tammie became very concerned, so she asked her what was going on with her and demanded she told her the truth. She asked her if it was anything that she could do to help her because she felt like Sanity was hiding something from her.

Catherine had her moments where she would bother Sanity nonstop but when she would stop it would be for months at a time. She felt like what Catherine was doing slowly became harassment and she felt herself losing her mind, so she turned to church even more. She would sit in church and not hear what the pastor was saying because she would zone out as soon as the music started playing. All the evil things Catherine said to her would play over and over in her head during church service. That's when she knew that Catherine was getting the best of her and from what she learned in church was not the type of faith she displayed. After Tammie asked Sanity so many times what was going on with her, Sanity decided to show and tell her everything that Catherine was taking her through. Sanity wasn't the type to tell anyone what Catherine was doing to her because Catherine had already told everyone not to believe her since she was younger. Tammie couldn't do anything but cry. She looked at Sanity and shook her head from side to side very slowly. She asked her why she didn't tell her what she was going through with her mother. She said had she knew she would have never dealt with her if she knew that she was that type of woman to her own child and grandchildren.

During that tax season Sanity saved up enough money to buy her another car her and Tammie was so excited that she was finally able to take her kids to and from daycare and school all on her own. It made Tammie so happy because the more Sanity would refuse rides, the more she saw Sanity struggle with getting her children around. There were days she would come in to work late and wet from the rainy weather. When Sanity got her new car, she wouldn't see Tammie most days until she got to work because they were no longer riding to work together, but that didn't stop them from goofing off every chance they got. They couldn't stay away from each other so there were days Sanity agreed she wouldn't drive and would have Tammie pick her up.

Sanity had gotten used to letting Tammie know everything that was going on with her, so it was so much easier for her to pick up the phone late nights or before daybreak in the morning to let Tammie know that Catherine was on a roller coaster again. Sanity made up in her mind that she just wasn't going to deal with Catherine. She was just going to pray for her and move on with her life with her children because Catherine had already caused more harm than good.

Catherine found other ways to get to Sanity she befriended Tammie behind Sanity's back and by the time she found out about it, it had been four years. She would tell Tammie to never trust Sanity and all Sanity did was lied about everything. She manipulated Tammie to believe everything Sanity had ever told her about her was a lie and the whole family knew Sanity was a liar. She even told Tammie that Sanity talked about her and her kids every chance she got, knowing that Sanity loved those kids as her own. A lot of what Catherine did destroyed Tammie's life as well because she texted Tammie over the years telling her things that Sanity said about her. She also texted Sanity from time to time and told her that Tammie said some of the most horrible things a friend could say about her and her children. Catherine got so bad with it she even went to Keisha bragging about the horrible things that she told Tammie about Sanity. When Tammie came to Sanity to apologize for listening to Catherine, it was too late because Sanity felt like one of the closest people to her had been manipulated into crossing her with the devil. She just couldn't believe Tammie waited years to tell her when they talked about everything including Catherine's abusive ways towards her.

TeTe tried talking Sanity into hearing Tammie out because they had become so close. She also told Sanity there were always two sides to every story. Sanity decided to meet up with Tammie after she sent an apologetic letter to her house. When she read the letter, she cried because she loved Tammie and she knew that Tammie loved her too. A part of Sanity wanted to say she was done with her but her heart and love for Tammie's children wouldn't let her, so she texted her and told her that they needed to have a serious sit down. Tammie knew exactly what it was about because two years went by without them speaking.

Later that day they met up and it was a much-needed conversation. Tammie told Sanity that she was about to lose her mind because when she tried not speaking to Catherine at all it was almost like she became obsessed with hurting Sanity. She would tell Tammie new lies everyday claiming she spoke to Sanity and years passed without Sanity even speaking to her. Sanity had officially cut her off for good. Sanity showed Tammie her phone and the messages that she received from Catherine over the years begging her to let her back into her life. She even showed messages from other family members telling Sanity that she only has one mother. Even though Tammie showed her proof of everything, she knew it was never her intentions to hurt Sanity. What bothered Sanity so bad was the fact that Tammie saw for herself what Catherine was taking her through, and she still fell for her lies. In all honesty, Sanity never stopped loving Tammie; she had to dig deep inside of her heart and realize why and how they became friends in the first place. She just decided to take a break from the friendship so that she could get herself together because she felt like she wasn't a great friend. Sanity walked around with a big smile on her face telling jokes all day, she was always the life of the party. But if only the party knew how deeply wounded she was.

Chapter 35

Sanity received a phone call from Keisha one day telling her that she was feeling a bit concerned about Big Momma's health. Sanity immediately got worried and started asking more questions looking for answers right then and there. In that conversation, she learned that while Big Momma's brain was going through changes, Catherine was still living her life to the fullest with her husband's family. The whole family including all of Catherine's siblings were stressing over who would be available for what times to sit with Big Momma so that she could be monitored because her memory was fading away fast. Sanity told Keisha she noticed the last time she had spoken to Big Momma she repeatedly asked her some of the same questions. She reached out to one of her Aunts that Big Momma was living with at the time and she said she thought that Big Momma's memory was declining because some days she would remember everything clearly but other days she would forget everything.

"Keisha I was in denial the last time I spoke to Big Momma," Sanity said. "She was all over the place with some of her words but when I called her back the next day, she was fine. A small part of me knew she was experiencing memory loss. The only reason I knew is because I see it a lot on my job," Sanity said as her voice started to crack. She didn't want to believe Big Momma was getting closer to being freed. No one understood why Catherine's absence was at the center of every conversation when it came to Big Momma. Catherine screamed to every sister and brother that called her about helping the family out with Big Momma so that she wouldn't be stuck at home or placed in a nursing home to just decline alone. Sanity and Keisha expressed their feelings to each other about Catherine turning her back on everyone she called on for everything. They couldn't understand how Big Momma raised every last one of Catherine's kids and got that type of treatment in the end.

"Sanity this is not right," Keisha said as she fought to hold back her tears.

"Yeah, I know, and this is another reason I don't visit often because Catherine will forever be self-centered and that will never change." Sanity was so angry during that phone call. She wanted to tell all of Catherine's old secrets, but she didn't because Keisha also heard Catherine's name being tossed around in many conversations and the sad part about it was the conversations were based off of how horrible she talked about her kids and grandkids. Finally, Sanity told Keisha she would have to call her back but what she didn't tell her was that she was going to call Catherine to tell her how she truly felt about the things she heard. The reason Sanity didn't tell Keisha what she was about to do was because Keisha wouldn't have believed it. That was the part of Sanity's life she wanted to stay as far away from the family as possible. Everyone in their family knew Sanity wouldn't go to her hometown unless a family member had passed away to show her respect. Catherine knew exactly why Sanity stayed away but kept quiet.

"Hello," with a soft-spoken voice Catherine answered.

"Hey," Sanity said with a very dry voice. This was the last person she wanted to have a conversation with especially after she had been sending her text messages talking about her other children, explaining to Sanity she really needed to talk to her. She didn't want anyone to know what she wanted to talk to her about as Sanity received the unanswered messages, she continued to read them. That's when she noticed there was never an apology in any of the messages for her but there were a lot of messages talking down on the rest of her siblings. Sanity didn't repeat any of it but before Catherine's cover was blown, she would call the other kids and tell them that she had an actual conversation with Sanity and flipped everything on her. She had Sanity's other siblings calling Sanity every name they could think of because they believed their mother. She rejoiced in leaving that same distance between the siblings because of her twisted lies. No matter how much Sanity cried out that she didn't speak to Catherine and it was made up lies no one wanted to hear her side of anything so that added on to her staying away.

"Hey Sanity, " Catherine said, sounding like she was sick with a cold.

"I wanted to call and see what's going on with Big Momma? Also, I want to know what the fuss is about all of her children that live local splitting days and times to sit with her because of her memory loss?"

"Look Sanity! I'm sick of all y'all calling me about this. I 've been with Big Momma all of my life and I took good care of her so now it's their turn to do it."

"What the hell do you mean?" Sanity said out of complete anger, "it ain't no way you're really saying this right now! How are you going to sit there and say you took good care of Big Momma and she was never sick so how? You're saying that you took good care of Big Momma, but I just can't understand how you could say that because she was never even sick for anyone to take care of her. In fact, she raised your kids, so I don't see what the big fuss is about." Catherine then started putting the blame on everyone but herself she said everything that she could have during that conversation, but she never gave in to helping out with Big Momma. Sanity told her she had to end the call because she was at work. Sanity felt like she didn't get anywhere with trying to talk to Catherine about her absence in Big Momma's life when she needed her the most. It made Sanity even more upset because she knew that if it was Catherine who needed the help without a doubt Big Momma would have been there even if she had to pay someone else to be there. After that conversation, it really had Sanity in a bad mood. She tried everything she could to get her mind off of what part could she have played in making sure that Big Momma was okay without having to be in town. She knew the odds were against her because it would have been almost impossible for her to have been there.

As the days went by, Sanity cried knowing that there was no way she could go to her hometown and be with Big Momma every day all day, as she wanted to. One day Sanity's kids asked if they could go over to Tammie's house to spend time with her kids because they weren't allowed to hang out with kids from the neighborhood that they were living in. She looked at her son's smile and replied to them by saying, "y'all didn't even have to ask me that!" She also reminded them no matter what Tammie's children would always be their family.

After a long stressful day at work, Sanity decided to go home and rest up before she picked the boys up from Tammie's house. After taking a long hot shower Sanity laid across her bed to take a nap before it was time but before she could fall asleep her phone rang. Her little sister told her that Big Momma wasn't doing well at all and that she needed to come home to visit her at the hospital. Sanity didn't ask what happened or why Big Momma was in the hospital; she started screaming at the top of her lungs because she knew things had taken a turn for the worse. She couldn't stand the thought of losing her even though she knew that Big Momma had lived a good prosperous life. Everything she did for her and her siblings was very well appreciated but yet still Sanity didn't care how old Big Momma was; she still felt like the world still had a place for her and that she would be around forever.

Sanity got herself together and called Tammie to let her know she wasn't going to be able to pick the boys up because she needed to get on the road to check on her grandmother. Tammie knew how much Sanity's grandmother meant to her so she told her that even when she got back to leave the boys with her, and she would make sure that they got to school the next day. Driving back to her hometown sent chills through her body every time she had to go there. She always felt the spirit of depression, anxiety or she just had a very sad feeling in her heart that she couldn't explain but once she got there of course she played it off as if she was always okay, but the truth was Sanity was never okay. Every step she took while she was there felt as if it was opening up old wounds. Sanity knew through it all she had to be there for Big Momma because she never ever let her down or turned her back on her before no matter what. She knew it was a must for her to be there. Sanity walked into the hospital to see her grandmother and the moment she walked into the room and saw a Big Momma just lying there she wanted to cry but she held back tears because Catherine was standing there with her arms folded. She looked as sad as she could. Sanity looked at Catherine and saw the look on her face. It was a look of disappointment not in Big Momma, but she often wondered could it have been in herself.

As the weeks went by, Big Momma didn't seem to get any better. The family was very sad. They bickered over who did what for Big Momma and Sanity was amongst the crowd. She went weeks beating herself up about the situation and she kept trying to come up with different ways to maneuver her life around being there for Big Momma more. At the end of the day, it all fell right back on all of her reasoning for not being there. Sanity lost more than she knew and didn't want to take any chances on losing anything or anyone else, especially her mind. Throughout life she felt like her mind was the only thing that she had left and she prayed hard to make sure that she never lost that. She also made promises to God that she would always do what she needed to do to protect her peace throughout the rest of her life.

Sanity sat quietly in a corner at work and as she was charting on one of her patients. All she could do was think about Big Momma but in her heart, she knew that it was time for her to go on and rest. It was that one little part of Sanity's heart that wasn't quite ready to let go of her and that's when she received the worst call of her life from her Aunt. She said she needed to rush back home to see Big Momma for the last time because the doctors had just left her hospital room from telling them that Big Momma wasn't going to make it throughout the week and all of her family needed to be near her bedside. "Oh my God! No! Oh my God no!" All she knew was that she was experiencing that same feeling when she got the call about Tim's death it was that feeling she never wanted to feel again. She fell all over the floor of her workplace asking, "God why? Why so soon?" In Sanity's mind she thought she had more time with Big Momma.

She ran out as fast as she could once a few of her coworkers were able to calm her down. It was one of the hardest things that she had to explain to her kids. Once she got home from work, she just laid out on the floor and didn't move. When they got home, they saw that she was laying in the corner of her bedroom floor balled up crying in tears. Losing Big Momma was like losing her biological mother. Everything she learned as a little girl up until her adult years she learned it from Big Momma. Sanity spent more time in her hometown-listening to all of the details and plans for Big Momma going away service. Sanity thought it was very special and important for the family to get together to make sure that Big Momma was laid to rest like the queen that she was. Surprisingly on the days Sanity was there, Catherine's attitude wasn't the same; she was more normal than she had ever been in her life. Sanity had small conversations with Catherine trying to feel her out, wanting to see if her heart and her mind had changed over the years.

The day finally came, it was time to say their last goodbyes to the heart of their entire family, Big Momma. On that day, Sanity almost lost her mind. She cried, screamed, and kicked as she walked down the isles to view Big Momma's body for the last time. She held onto Big Momma's casket and wouldn't let go of it until her three Aunts walked up to her. One of them whispered in her ear to tell her it was okay to let Big Momma rest on. Sanity kept screaming. After Sanity's Aunts nearly dragged her back to her seat to sit down so that she could catch a breath, she looked over her right shoulder and noticed that Catherine was just looking around as if she didn't exist at all. Sanity knew Catherine of all people knew how much she loved Big Momma and how much Big Momma loved her back. Not one time did she get up to hold Sanity to tell her everything was going to be okay, she ignored her and that was the moment Sanity never looked at her the same.

Sanity found ways to deal with her childhood trauma by helping others who went through some of the same type of situations. Her helping others gave her more strength each day. Early on in her life she was putting the blame on herself thinking she should have acted a certain way once she got tired of the abuse and mistreatment. When she decided to close the door when it came to the mistreatment, name calling, and giving Catherine money, it gave her a sense of power. It was a power she knew she had but just needed a way to find it. Sanity spent her entire life wanting love from her mother, the type of love her mother couldn't and wasn't willing to give her. It was clear Catherine didn't love herself and if a person can't love themself enough to be a great mother to their children, then they can't love anyone else. It starts with loving yourself and finding out who you really are, admitting your wrongs and living in your truth. In the end, Sanity allowed Catherine to control so much of her life so many miles away but one thing she didn't do was give up. Hope and faith is what got her where she is today.

The thoughts of her ending her life is something she doesn't experience anymore because she decided to claim her life back. Regardless of who it is or how it may hurt, you have to find your peaceful place and stay there. Mental health is real, and it is important. Being silent doesn't help but it does hurt more if you stay silent. Just because you speak up doesn't make you any less of a person, but what it does is make you a leader.

Abandonment and neglect happen inside of people's homes everyday more often than we know. Just because a child lives in the home with the parents doesn't mean it's not considered abandonment or neglect if a parent is mentally and emotionally abusive. We must make sure the cycle doesn't continue. It is our job to say something before it destroys other's lives. Sanity took pride in the platforms she was offered to speak on, because she knows the pain of not having an outlet to run to. Her voice needed to be heard so she could spread love and awareness to anyone that needs it. Sanity closed the door to the pain in her life. Because of that pain, she has an open-door policy for helping others heal.

Dedications

So now you've gotten a fair chance to get to know the real Sanity. After all Sanity has been through, she is happily married to a man that knew exactly what she was dealing with when he met her, but he never gave up or judged her. Pushing him away was not an option. He remained patient with her. He stuck around and got to meet the real Sanity. They now have a total of five children, four of their own, one they adopted from the same type of pain of Sanity's past and one beautiful granddaughter. They are still healing each other each day.

In Loving Memory
Dameon Nova (Tim)
&
Lucia Nova (Big Momma)

About the Author

My name is Qunetta Davis, formally known as Qunetta Wannamaker. I am 39-years-old, a loving wife, mother of three young men, and grandmother of one beautiful granddaughter. I grew up in the very small city of Orangeburg, S. C. with a never ending passion for helping people, as we took on poverty by a storm. I started out at the age of 11 wanting to be a star. I had a strong passion for music and acting, something that wasn't a priority growing up in the low country. Back then, you had to live for each day and not spend too much time focusing on your future. Many families struggled and dealt with a lot of dis functional events right inside of their homes, but never spoke on it. This was either because they were told not to, or were just too scared. For many families, this resulted in mental health issues. The same issues that lead to drug abuse, sexual abuse, child abuse, and physical abuse. After experiencing traumatic events of my own, I entered the medical field, becoming a Certified Nursing Assistant at the age of 18-years-old. After a long battle with depression and anxiety, I decided to use my voice loud and clear so that I can give back to my very own community, and to anyone anywhere who wants their voice heard. After a tragedy took place in my life, I gave up on my dreams to battle with my own demons. I did a lot of soul searching, ultimately realizing that what I went through wasn't my fault, because I was only a child during my traumatic experiences. Everyone had part in telling my story except me, due to the code of not speaking up. Today, because of the lifestyle I was forced to live, I am now the author of my own story.